AF615953

Permission

RETURNING TO THE GOD-CREATED YOU

Dr. Jackie Greene

Copyright © 2018 by Dr. Jackie Greene.

All rights reserved. No part of this publication may be reproduced, distributed or transmitted in any form or by any means, including photocopying, recording, or other electronic or mechanical methods.

Permission / Dr. Jackie Greene. —1st ed.
ISBN 978-0-578-43086-7

Contents

Foreword ... *v*
Dedication ... *vii*
Introduction ... *ix*
I. Chapter One-ATLANTA: Born into Truth
A. The Early Years ... 1
B. Daddy's Girl ... 7
C. Momma, Why? ... 10

II. Chapter Two-SANDERSVILLE: The First Thing Became Second
A. Living Up to the Hype ... 13
B. Midnight Milk Run ... 21

III. Chapter Three-STATESBORO: I Woke Up
A. I Took It All Off ... 27
B. He Set Me on Fire ... 30
C. Nerd Jackie ... 31
D. One Question Changed It All ... 34
E. When Good Isn't Good Enough ... 39
F. Travis Meets Kathy ... 41

IV. Chapter Four-AUGUSTA: Stepping into the New
A. He Broke Me to Rebuild Me ... 45
B. Circle of Love ... 51
C. Sixty-Three Days in Bed ... 52
D. We Birthed a Miracle ... 60

V. Chapter Five-CHARLOTTE: New Beginnings
A. Home Sweet Home ... 63
B. The Call ... 67

VI. Chapter Six-COLUMBIA: New Levels
A. Moving Forward ... 71
B. The Champ Is Here! ... 75
C. Real Talk. Real Work. ... 77
D. The Rebirth of Dr. JG ... 84

Statement of Permission ... 89

FOREWORD

What if you had a blank check from a billionaire to pay for your dreams? What if your friends were the world's greatest athletes, movie stars, and cultural icons? What if you had superhuman powers to fly, teleport, and kick down walls? At least one of these "what if's" has crossed your mind before. Let's face it, all of these advantages would be awesome! It would certainly make life a lot easier. I have one more "what if." What if none of these "advantages" were really the things limiting or blocking you from walking in God's purpose for your life?

I have a secret to tell you. Shhh... This is highly classified information. Wait, before I tell you this secret, let me first reveal the source behind the secret. There's a woman I met several years ago. Don't get me wrong, she was always Amazing. I had no clue that she could become more Amazinger. She discovered this secret that I'm about to tell you and it unlocked the most Amazingliest parts of her. As you can tell, real words can't describe her Amazingnessibilities. Sorry, back to the secret. You ready?

Here's the secret I learned from the woman who wrote the book you're holding. There's one thing that a blank check can't afford. It's more significant than your network. It's a force greater than any mutant superpowers. The secret to your wildest dreams coming true is understanding that God has already given you permission! Hold on, so you mean I don't have to wait any longer to be who I was created to be? Exactly! The wait is over. The secret is out. Once you discover the permission you've been granted, striving will cease. This book eliminates the excuses that have caged you into "Someday Land." Someday I'll do this and someday I'll become that. That day has arrived; the time is now. As you read this book, layers of false identity will peel back with every page you turn. Get ready to walk in power, passion, and purpose.

Destiny awaits. Permission is given. Move forward.

–Travis Greene

DEDICATION

This book means so much to me. I give honor to God for every word He allowed to comprise the fullness of my story. Daddy, You never cease to amaze me, and I thank You for the finished work You did on Calvary that afforded me the freedom that I now stand in. I take this moment also to honor my mom and dad for birthing me. This book is dedicated to you because without you it would not have been possible. Mom, thank you for being such an amazing example for me. You have been right there every step of the way! I am the product of good heritage, and I thank you both for all that you are to me. Daddy Willie, thank you for stepping in to love me as if I were your own. I honor you as well. I dedicate this book to every family member, friend, and mentor who helped shape me into the woman I have become. Your love, support, and consistency will never be forgotten. I have to personally thank my best friend Keshia. Without you, this book would still be a great idea for the future. You pushed me to get it done. I am forever grateful for you. Norman and Blair, thank you for devoting your lives to helping us see through each vision God blesses Travis and me with. You both treat it as an honor and not a task; it means more than you know. To my in-house editing team (Dr. Karla, Sway, Crystal, Brittney, Bridgett, and Jamez) and my village that helps with the boys, thank you! You are my voices of encouragement, the readers of my rough ideas, and the hands that aid in nurturing my most prized possessions. To my editor, Janice Brown, you took my hand and helped me to believe in moments where I had given up, Thank you! Your investment is eternal. Jace and Josh, I pray that witnessing your mom and dad live what they preach will inspire you both to live your truth as well. I am forever blessed to be the mother of such incredible sons! Momma Greene, Kim, and Shalonda, thank you for helping to present to me such a marvelous gift in my husband. I am grateful for each of you and the role you have played in my becoming. Last but not least, I offer Permission as a gift to my husband, who has seen my truth since the day we met when I was only nineteen. Baby, you have been patient with me and loved me as much on my good days as my bad. You have always honored me, and you chose me above all others to stand as your bride. I thank you for the way you have laid your life down for our family. I pray this book will serve as a testament of your ministry of freedom. I think it's super dope to go all around the world and effect change, but it demonstrates the ultimate level of power when you effect change in your own home! You have helped change my life for the better. You beat down the walls that once caged me in. With the authority given by God, you dared me to live my real life! This is your story as much as it is mine. Thank you for helping me see that I have full PERMISSION and for loving my truth!

"Am I now trying to win the approval of human beings, or of God? Or am I trying to please people? If I were still trying to please people, I would not be a servant of Christ." —Galatians 1:10 NIV

INTRODUCTION

Where am I? Am I alive? Am I upside down? I do a mental check while trying to adjust to my surroundings. I'm still in my car. It's so dark! It's after midnight and I'm on an empty road in small-town Georgia, but how did I get here?

Slowly the realization of what just happened came through like flashes of light. We had a fight. I was driving home. I fell asleep. I almost died! As I crawled out of my brand-new convertible, a gift for being a dependable daughter, the weight of my current circumstances was revealed. I snuck my boyfriend home, while my mom was working night shift. We had a fight where he ended up throwing stuff. I took him home, but I was exhausted. After falling asleep, my car flipped multiple times. God spared me! Somehow, I survived!

As I walked down this dark road in the middle of the night, my thoughts became more intense. God, have I lived a life that made You proud? Have I even lived the life that You intended? Have I lived my true life and been my true self? The answers deepened the disappointment that I was already carrying. Who am I? I know on the outside everything looks picture- perfect, but "World," you demanded this of me. You told me to fake it till I make it! If I'm broken, I'm supposed to act as if I'm whole. If I'm unsure, act as if I know it all. Never show my real truth.

Does any of this sound familiar to you? We wear the persona of perfection so well. From the moment we wake up, we begin this journey to prove to everyone around us that we have it all together. We must, at all cost, uphold this image that everyone expects of us. Our people-pleasing day begins with posting the ideal breakfast on social media. (Only to put down our phones and eat the donut that we wouldn't want anyone to know we had.) Next, we go through a series of internal conversations trying to decide which outfit and hairstyle will impress those we come in contact with most. We snap our selfie on the way to the job that we hate but continue to use as a cover, for without it, we're not sure people will still think we're making "big moves." After making it through a day of misery, we settle for a dinner date with someone who's far from a long-term candidate, but better than loneliness. Not to mention what our family would think if we didn't have a serious relationship, heading toward marriage, by the age of thirty.

Truth be told, we live in a world of imperfection. From the moment we take our first breath, we enter a life that we are not privileged to hand-select. So often, we are left to cope with the realities of what actually exists. Once we've been broken, it seems as if we willfully surrender the permission God granted us, the permission to become all that He uniquely destined us to be. We find ourselves living lives contrary to who we really are by trying to please the demands of the world around us. I want those reading this to recognize that you have the power and courage to snatch your permission back. You have the wherewithal to decide that. Yes, I went through "that" and it caused me to question "this," but I will not continue to live a life dictated by external forces.

At many points in my life, I found it a struggle to decide which image I would choose to take on. The one living a life that brings true fulfillment, though it may take hard work and not be as applauded by man; or the safe, superficial version that moves from season to season in search of another thing to satisfy its lack of contentment. The battle of where we seek our permission from is constant. The world demands that we look to it to serve us the validation we need via our social media following, the number of likes on our recent post, new job titles, our relationship status, or compliments we receive throughout the day. But the world, it seems, can only offer us an external affirmation that is fleeting. This is just a substitute for time that should be spent with the Father, where He will truly affirm and secure our identity in Him.

You are about to enter my life's journey on how God awakened the reality that although life happens and the world may make its demands, I have already been granted full permission to be the "ME" that He created. I don't think there is anything more disheartening in life than knowing that there is a more bold, free, anointed version of yourself locked away inside this counterfeit person you've settled for. This was my story for way too long, but I'm grateful to say it was not my end! **My shift came only after reestablishing the fact that my permission didn't come from the world around me, but from the God within me.** As children, we are introduced to the need to gain permission before we do anything. We often retain that childlike need, until we come to realize that just as God matures us to stop needing permission to go potty, speak, or eat; such is the road to freely live our real life. Gradually, we begin to own that we are **B**old, **A**nointed, and **D**estined-to-win! Yes, we are all BAD girls and boys, and we didn't just become BAD! From the moment our amazing Father births us, everything we are to become is already in us!

I'm so excited for those of you who have decided to take this journey with me. I must warn you that the journey to live your truth is not for the faint of heart. Radical faith, tenacity, and many tear-filled-snotty-nose nights have accompanied me on this road. I pray that you would be willing to let go of everything you once knew to allow God to reintroduce the authentic you to the world. Everything I thought I knew about me or what comprised my identity, God either stripped or purified. This book displays a road map of how God peeled back the layers to uncover who I have always been, and He wants to do the same for you. It's funny how the process of becoming is more of an undoing and unlearning rather than the contrary. You have already been given full permission to find your voice and live your truth. I dare you to LIVE! Here's my story on how I finally started!

Chapter One

ATLANTA: Born into Truth

"Start children off on the way they should go, and even when they are old they will not turn from it."
—Proverbs 22:6 NIV

THE EARLY YEARS

In the 1980s, God orchestrated the collision of two drastically different individuals. In a drugstore in the great city of Atlanta, Ga., Dr. Yaw Adu Gyamfi, a man of West African descent, met a sweet ol' country girl named Cynthia Harris, from the small town of Sandersville, Ga. They exchanged information and the rest was history. The two young pharmacists married, settled, and began a life together, with each playing such a profound role in laying a sure foundation for me. Growing up, their contributions looked very different to me, but it is clear to see how much they both imparted, as I look back from a mature perspective. With my parents both having huge hearts for people, they each set out with great ambition to make an impact in every place God called them.

My dad has always had global vision and macro ideas, believing that he could achieve anything he set out to do. My mom is one to maximize every moment. She never saw any opportunity to impact another's life as too small. As a result, the two birthed a pharmacy together in Atlanta, which served our local community. All my life I have seen my mom treat those who the world would see as "the least of these" with such dignity and honor. Whether it was her pausing a busy schedule to tend to another, paying for bus fares, or taking her patients grocery shopping, I have always seen the example of being the true hands and feet of Jesus modeled through her everyday life. I feel that I have become a melting pot of both of their perspectives, and it has allowed me to love and lead people well, owning the beauty of what God allowed them to instill in me.

I am the second child they were blessed with, coming behind my older brother, Norman Kofi Gyamfi. He is one of the world's greatest gifts, a natural-born genius! He is still a work in progress, as we all are , but the lasting imprint he will make on this world will be profound. My mom and dad were very active members of a local ministry—*The Settled Word Ministries*, which provided a doorway for my brother and me to begin to serve and gain understanding of who God was at a very early age. I can vividly recall being extremely young and standing up in front of my whole church professing how grateful I was that God helped me make a 100% on my test and that He healed my headache. The irony in that is that it would be through academia that I would come to know God more personally later in my journey. It's so beautiful the way God reveals Himself even to children early on. I was the only toddler amidst an adult praise team, standing up singing songs with my whole heart to a God who is very real to me. My brother, at the age of four, mounted the pulpit to preach the message at our Sunday worship gathering at this church. It was this ministry that cemented an understanding of how unique and necessary the call of God was on our lives. This ministry believed in affirming the hand of God on one's life at an early age, which ingrained a huge hunger to get to know and love God with all of me, even as a child. This was the start of my recognizing that I already had God's permission to be who He had called me to be.

I was so bold and unapologetic about the way God made me! I gave no thought to what people would think or "what if I don't do this right!" It was as if failure wasn't an option, so I pursued all that I felt led by God to do. **I lived in the freedom of my truth. I was secure in who God was which in turn made me secure in who I am.** Have you ever stopped to consider where your security lies? Do you believe that your life is secured by the job you currently have or the amount of money you earn? Do you feel as if having that job or amount of money is the thing that sets you apart, gives you significance, and allows you to face life's uncertainties without fear? I know many of us find ourselves here at various points in our lives. Lots of us go through phases of believing that things that have no bearing on our real identity are primary to who we really are. We may never verbally admit it, but the truth of it shows up when layoffs happen, relationships end, or a major life event occurs that alters our level of income. We find ourselves feeling as if we no longer have a reason to live or we feel worthless. These emotions emerge due to believing the lie that these things made us who we are.

It is so important that we are honest about what we believe comprises our identity, so that God is able to heal our misguided views. I often say based on my own life's journey, **God can't help what we hide!** This book is your opportunity to dig deep to find out what's really at your core. God isn't intimidated by what we find, no matter how silly it may seem. He just desires access! I am a living witness that **God will heal what we are brave enough to expose!** You will see this become more apparent as we journey forward, but in Atlanta I was settled in what God had to say about me.

I was ok with being the only one who looked and acted like me. I was young, passionate, and a genuine lover of Jesus. I think God was intentional about my initial encounters with Him happening during a time where I was fearless, affirmed, and encouraged to worship God from a fully surrendered place. I can't tell you the number of times, as I progressed through life, where I remembered back to those moments at *The Settled Word Ministries*. They helped define my early identity and a girl I would get to know again, later in life. I never paid attention to the name of my very first church until writing this book. It was called *The Settled Word Ministries*! God allowed me to begin my roots in a place that believed the Word that God speaks is a settled Word! WOW!

How did life begin for you? Does taking the moment to look back bring to light some ah-ha moments of your own? Can you recall a word that has been highlighted or affirmed about you over and over that began in your early days? Maybe a person of influence often spoke to your ability to lead, love, or create. Were you bold, fearless, or full of belief? How have you changed as you have grown and matured and learned more about the world around you? When reflecting back to the younger version of yourself, are there any characteristics that you wish you still exhibited? I've found when looking back on my early years that so many things changed as I moved through my journey of life.

We begin life so sure of ourselves. We learn that our voice makes noise and we make the loudest noise we can. We find out that walking isn't as hard as we thought, so we dare to start running! We sing without regard for who's listening. We love in a way that is so pure and genuine. **We believe in others with such a faith that it causes others to believe in themselves.** This is the childlike faith that wipes away the tears of our parents who are doubting if they are fully equipped to rear us well, because they sense the sureness we have in them. Our unwavering faith in our parents helps them to remember what they are made of, and that they can do the thing that they were designed to do in a way no one else can! The profound effect of sureness!

We are born an authentic, raw, choice treasure, fashioned by the hand of God. It's so amazing that when we're young, most of us are so daring. Can you remember the things you wore as a child? The purple and yellow polka-dot dress with the red rain boots you wore because it was your favorite outfit, and it made you happy. Or what about the Ninja Turtle shirt with the red and white striped shorts. You were only able to put this combination together because you were at home with your dad and knew he loved it when you exerted your independence to choose. **Before we are taught to be concerned with other people's opinion of us, we are free of the internal weight of other people's perception of who we are.** We are not void of the innate desire to make our parental figures proud of us, but **our whole life is not dictated by the hypotheticals of what someone else is thinking.**

Once we gain this awareness, life as we know it takes a drastic shift. We begin to live in a world where our internal space is inundated with "they and them" questions. Do "they" think i'm qualified enough? I wonder what "they" think I'm like? Are "they" ok with the decision I made? I wonder what "they" are saying when I'm not around? Will "they" even like my book? Swimming in a sea of hypotheticals we lose our courage to be and do what we would naturally be and do! We succumb to the pressures of our internal dialogue and invite the unwelcome guest known as "the world's permission" in to stay.

People-pleasing and wanting others' permission to be the YOU that God created is a nationwide epidemic, and we are in an all-out fight during this current era! It is one of the greatest attacks on the authentic, purpose-filled, free life! People-pleasing is a huge problem today, but I wouldn't want you to mistakenly think that this is an issue isolated to our present day. In Galatians 1:10, Paul makes clear that the war of pleasing people versus pleasing God dates all the way back to the first-century church. He declares that it is impossible to please people and be a servant of God! This is a powerful statement that makes so much sense about why the war to regain my permission meant so much to God! Did you know that people-pleasing could be that detrimental? It literally disturbs our relationship with the Father.

Sometimes I wonder how our life would be different if we would return back to the boldness and sureness of our youth? This audacity requires us to accept our quirkiness, love ourselves, and embrace the things that others may mock or have an opinion about. Has the reality that God had the ability to handcraft you any way He desired ever hit you? **The revelation that God designed me exactly the way He wanted me changed my life!** I beat myself up for so long because I talk fast, love hard, cry easily (especially with my Goddaughter Dajia), and have fine hair that doesn't grow as rapidly as many others. This is just to name a few things. You know we as humans will come up with it! Mad at life because our right big toe is slightly fatter than our left. We feel inadequate because that one tooth is half a millimeter longer than the other one, and decide to never smile. And let's not get started on why we don't talk like, love like, or have a shape like so-and-so! I came to recognize that all of these differences are what make me uniquely me. If God wanted any one of my emotional, physical, or personality traits to be different, He could have made it that way easily! I freed myself of the pressure of not wanting to be different and embraced my difference!

I'm so grateful that I have a mom who has always been fully vested in me being authentic! She would often remind me of my true identity when it was clear that I had lost grip of it. I can remember various times growing up hearing my mom say her infamous identity check line, "Jackie, you're not living from your heart!" Those words stopped me dead in my tracks. Although packaged in so much love, they brought with them such a harsh sting. You know how some words your parents say bounce around in your mind, as you roll your eyes to the rhythm at which you are used to hearing it? This line was not that type of correction. It was a command to immediately evaluate the action or behavior I was displaying, because it was not in line with my true identity. I could have been in the middle of nagging my older brother for attention, acting as if it was impossible for me to do anything on my own, or acting fearful about an upcoming endeavor. All my mom had to do was hit me with that one line, and I immediately knew my actions weren't reflecting my true heart. I ask you in this moment, "Are you living from your true heart?"

It's amazing how God will speak things to you in your youth that will still hold so much relevance in your present. **God's challenge to me, for as long as I can remember, is to live my truth.** I believe this challenge is a universal call of God to all of His children. He has such a desire for each of us to be genuine and authentic to the way He originally created us. For when the Father was done designing you, He saw a masterpiece! **What do you see?** This is such an important question to pause and answer! **Embracing God's version of ourselves is the only way to truly live in freedom.** The Word says the truth will set you free, and this is something that was so very evident in my early life.

My early life was filled with many things that were pivotal to my sure foundation. When we decide to share our stories, it is often important not only to bring to the table the positive things that shaped us but also the painful things that played a role. This allows others who have had to withstand the real blows of life the opportunity to see themselves in your personal details. It also creates a safe space for healing and real transparency to begin. It was in Atlanta that two very devastating attacks on my identity occurred. I would not know the full weight of these experiences until I began to see these breaches show up as areas of weakness in my life, season after season, as I moved from location to location.

DADDY'S GIRL

I have been told many times of the excitement that exuded from my father, on the fifteenth day of December 1987 at Decatur Hospital, when my mother gave birth to his first baby girl. It has been said that my older brother was somewhat of a momma's boy, so my dad was so excited when I arrived. I mentioned in the beginning that both my parents have always had a huge desire to make lasting impacts in the lives of others. The thing that complicated this situation a bit, from my point of view as a little girl, is that the people my father desired to impact most were the people of his homeland in Ghana, West Africa. Ghana was a land that I did not know very well, but my dad desired to bring innovative change to this area. It was a yearning that was very deeply rooted in his heart. In January of 1992, shortly after my fourth birthday, my mom and dad mutually decided for my father to return back to his homeland and fulfill his lifelong dream of establishing pharmaceutical businesses there to combat the leading causes of death for the African people (i.e., AIDS, malaria, and hepatitis). You see, although this is a very honorable cause, a four-year-old has no capacity to understand the pull he had to fulfill this noble vision. The only thing my brother and I knew is that our dad was once with us, and now he was gone. His departure left such a void inside of me. I had so many questions and things that I just couldn't quite understand for much of my life. How would my life have been different if my daddy stayed? Did he not love us? Were the people of his homeland more important than my brother and me? Why didn't we just go with him?

A year passed, and I was heading into kindergarten. We were on our way to school, and I can remember the car ride like it was yesterday. My mom randomly balled up some very important news and interjected it into our normal car conversation time. She said to Norman and me that she had filed for divorce. I remember both of us being very upset with her, feeling as if our whole world had come undone. Based on our response, it was clear that we still had high expectations for us to be together as one family again. Norman remarked back sharply, fighting through tears to my mom, "I'm going to tell my dad you divorced him when he calls again!" The fantasy of us all being one happy family again would remain just that for the rest of our lives—a fantasy.

It was all so confusing because I only had such good memories of my dad. He adored me! I remembered climbing up onto the bed and lying beside him with my head on his chest. I could always recall his big smile and extremely loud laugh. Even the times when he called us after going back to Ghana, it was always like Christmas for Norman and me. We would scream and jump up and down when we heard his voice on the line. He always referred to me as his Madame Abenaa Adansi, My Princess, or Mommy Jackie. His words were always filled with so much love.

My mom never spoke one negative word about my father. It seemed as if she fully understood his decision to go back to Africa, or if not fully understood, at least came to be ok with it. I never once sensed any anger or bitterness from my mom about him leaving. She did her best at every phase of our lives to help us navigate his absence. She is an absolute rock star. I already had enough challenges to deal with, just grappling with the loss of his presence, and I believe my mom's lack of negativity about my father helped me tremendously in the long run.

I remember every time I would come to her with questions about why my daddy left me, she would immediately remind me that my dad grew up in a different culture, one that is much different than the one I lived in. She would always try to help me see that his desire to go and do a thing that had never been done, to produce a legacy for my brother and me, was love to him. Being the eldest of ten children, my dad had always known the pressure of pioneering the way for those he loved behind him. I think he was just wired this way.

I went eight years, from age four to twelve, without ever seeing my dad's face. My brother and I went to visit Accra, Ghana, my sixth-grade summer. I was able to go and lay eyes on the pharmacies my dad had birthed. He had accomplished a portion of his call, but he was still pushing full steam ahead to add to the vision. When I visited, I gained a much better understanding as to just how drastically different the two worlds we live in are. It also became apparent that although we weren't a part of his daily life, we were always close to his heart. At his office one day I was able to see that he keeps a small picture of Norman and me in his Bible, and he uses that picture to pray over us daily. There was also a grocery store that he owned there named after Norman and me, and at every pharmacy we went to, each of his employees knew us by name and were so excited to meet us.

This life event wasn't one that I magically woke up one day healed from. You will see throughout my story many seasons where I battled with this daddy brokenness. I was a freshman in college before I even realized just how much about this situation I didn't know. I was asked to write a paper in my literature class about one of the most devastating things I had to live through. I found out through this paper that the decision for my father to move back to Africa was mutual between him and my mom. I know I mentioned it early on, but I didn't actually know this until college. I had always assumed that he just decided to leave with no consideration for us. Finding out in college that there had always been a plan to set up life in America and Ghana, though it never came to fruition, helped my heart heal tremendously. It didn't prevent the mistakes I made on the way to healing, but it did help me to realize that there are so many factors to be considered to fully understand how growing up without a dad present affected me. I think it would be unfair to try and speak for my father or mother on the subject. Maybe they will write their own book one day. Trying to fully understand was too much work and it distracted me from what I really needed. More than understanding I needed healing. I left the understanding to God and just began to try and live through it. I am aware that culture, marital tension, and family dynamics all played a role. This life event took a heavy blow at my sure identity that God had been so careful to create and establish so early on. This moment was just the first identity attack, and the second had just as significant an impact on my life.

MOMMA, WHY?

I remember as a little girl playing dress up. I would put on my mom's red or pink lipstick, grab a pair of her high heels, and find her most beautiful set of earrings. I loved the long dangly kind. I would swing my head back and forth, saying to my mom, "Ooh, Ma, you gotta give me these!" I was always so mature for my age. As I looked in the mirror back then I recall my hair going through so many crazy phases. I didn't even make it to my second birthday with my natural hair intact. You may be thinking, "What?!" At this point you might be tempted to become very judgmental toward my momma.

LOL! My momma told my brother and me that our hair was unmanageable as children. Let's just say we had very tight curls back in a day when natural hair products or knowledge on how to manage natural hair was not prevalent the way it is today. Regardless, may I just insert, before I paint the full picture of what happened, that my momma knows she was wrong for doing this to me.

My mom got the bright idea to relax my hair before I even turned two. As if that wasn't good enough, she unknowingly decided a few years later to add a texturizer to my hair to mix with the relaxer. She didn't know that the texturizer was a chemical as well. The combination sounds like a recipe for a disaster, right? That's exactly what it was. The sad thing is that the young girl attached to that disaster was little girl Jackie. I learned from a very young age that my hair was a part of me that was never good enough. I never had a chance to learn normalcy in this area. All I ever knew was damage and discontentment. I suffered the ridicule of my brother and various others as they watched bald spots form due to the two chemicals not agreeing. I remember being so self-conscious about my hair even as a little girl.

Can you envision the way this situation scarred my ability to believe in the purity of my natural beauty? On the surface this could read as a mere insult to my physical appearance, but it was so much deeper. I don't think there was a part of me that this hair situation didn't touch. I struggled emotionally, spiritually, and physically. Due to it occurring so early in life, it made me feel as if this was a part of my identity. It was as if this hair episode came and bulldozed a hole into my sure foundation, and made clear that it was here to stay. It created just enough space for me to begin to doubt my sureness. Which is all the enemy needs—to use you against yourself. I was my own worst critic and I believed every hypothetical I was presented with.

I'm sure many of you can relate. Pausing for just a moment might bring to mind things in your early life that came to rob you of innocence and strip you of true identity. You will hear a ton more about my struggles with this trauma even after its initial occurrence. This had to be one of the biggest giants I fought in life. It dealt me some heavy blows, but triumph is the inheritance of royal sons and daughters!

My mom is my shero! She may not have gone to hair school, but she is without question the biggest reason I have become who I am today, with the leading of God, of course! After the transition of my father to Ghana, we remained in Atlanta for about two more years. With the help of one of my most beloved great-aunts, Auntie Doll, my mom continued to rear us in the Word while being a full-time working woman, mommy, daddy, and whatever else my brother and I needed her to be. If there is one cause to which my mom has given absolutely her all, it is being a mother to my brother and me. Around that second year of being a single mother in Atlanta, my mom felt it best to relocate us to her hometown where she would gain the unconditional support of her mom, my Grandma Katie! It was here that we had a very large family willing and ready to love my brother and me, helping us to continue charting our way through life as my mom transitioned our life from Atlanta. Shout-outs to all the many family members who stepped in looking for nothing in return, who helped my mom and grandma continue to nurture Norman and myself. Let's head on over to Sandersville, a place that helped me write a completely different narrative than that of my time in Atlanta.

Chapter Two

SANDERSVILLE: The First Thing Became Second

"Don't copy the behavior and customs of this world, but let God transform you into a new person by changing the way you think. Then you will learn to know God's will for you, which is good and pleasing and perfect."
—Proverbs 22:6 NIV

LIVING UP TO THE HYPE

I spent twelve years of my life in my mother's hometown of Sandersville, Georgia, a place known for its southern hospitality. It is a very small town hosting a population of approximately six thousand people. It is known as the Kaolin Capital of the world. For those of you who are wondering to yourself, "What is Kaolin?" It is a white chalk-like material used for a wide variety of things, ranging from making paper to helping blood clot. In this small town, everybody knows everybody. When I grew up, it was a place where you would leave your doors unlocked, and you didn't leave your house without expecting to know almost every person with whom you came in contact.

Sandersville is all about the small-town way. The highlight of the week was Friday night football or basketball games. It has a main road that runs through much of its square footage commonly known as *The Four Lane*. It is a place where the upgrade from a standard Walmart to a Super Walmart is huge. Due to the lack of shopping malls or large chain restaurants, Walmart was the place to be for socializing and leisure when I was growing up. It's so much fun to think back on your roots. With all of its positives, **the good ol' country way also lent itself to a life where every detail of your existence was the business of every resident.** Having left the large city of Atlanta as a six-year-old, where I was very sheltered, Sandersville was a much different way of life. My life in Atlanta was church, home, school, and family. We knew very few people, and very few people knew us. Sandersville was the polar opposite.

My mom was fortunate to have a mother who lived a life of sacrifice and benevolence. So, joining forces with her to raise us was a no-brainer. She has always been so good to us. She helped rear Norman and me as if we were her own. She is such a unique lady in that she is a woman of very few words. However, if she gets going about something, you better pull up a seat to listen. She always pointed us to the higher road. I was taught to honor and respect my elders by this amazing woman. She also emphasized the importance of getting a good education. She took us to church every second and fourth Sunday for as long as we lived with her. I watched her during every service and imitated her mannerisms, hoping to become even slightly as phenomenal as she was in my eyes. She is another one of my sheroes, one who has played an invaluable role in my life of becoming.

Due to the greatness embodied by my grandma and all the prominence she held in our community, I stepped into a life where everything I said or did mattered. There were always eyes of scrutiny watching. Being under a microscope resulted in a lot of pressure for me. I had only lived for the approval of God and parents, prior to this phase. I loved people, but it was hard to contend with all the opinions. Maybe you know what that feels like. Having a huge heart for others is most definitely a gift, but this gift aided in the devastation of my real identity during this period of my life. **I had so much to prove to everybody that it actually kept me from living at all.** It wasn't an intentional thing.

I want each of you to know that you can end up losing your freedom to live without even intending to do so. I've found that we can be alive, waking up and going to sleep each day, but not truly be living. True life is synonymous with freedom to be who God has created you to be. With that in mind, would you say you are truly living? Or do you exist in a life that is fully dictated by the rules of what society says, living up to the expectations of others, or even the false realities that you may have accepted as "who you really are"? Are you doing this because some life happening broke your real identity, and made you feel that settling for what everybody else likes is the only real life you will know? This was definitely the case for me.

My priority for pleasing God and being who He had authentically created me to be was sidetracked by wanting to be perfect so that maybe my dad would see it and decide I was worth coming back for. I wanted all those around me to know that I didn't think I was better. Because of who my grandma was, that assumption was a very well-known preconceived notion about members of my family. I can remember being as young as elementary school and being taunted by girls saying, "Jackie Gyamfi thinks she's all that," or, "She thinks she's pretty." It was a thing from as early as I can remember. Being that this wasn't my heart, I felt an extra undue burden to prove everyone who thought that wrong. I tried to make myself be normal so that I could fit in and be liked by everyone. This seems so trivial now, but in the world of an elementary student it was a real thing, much like the thing you feel you have to prove to the world in your life right now. Maybe you are fixated on being seen as a great mom, a ride-or-die girlfriend, or a boss in your sphere of influence. The emphasis being shifted to prove these things can actually steal the freedom to be authentically who you are. I found this out the hard way. **We have to be so careful to guard our truth, for even the slightest shift in focus can rob us of it!**

People-pleasing and looking to "they and them" for permission before I did anything began the creation of a person far different from who I really was. Don't get me wrong, I think God allowed a few people while in Sandersville to truly know the real me, but even then, it was only a portion of who I was, because I was still learning my truth during this time. Some of my closest friends and family, like Renaldo, Sierra, and even one of my mentors, Mrs. Stephens, had some idea of the real me. I don't think any of them are shocked by who I've become. Taking an overall look at the theme of who I was and what life was about while in Sandersville, I would overwhelmingly scream, "COUNTERFEIT!" The vast majority were exposed to a false version of me. I'm sure many of you can relate to a time where you totally lost yourself. This is exactly where I was!

I set out on my journey to uphold the standard of perfection and excellence. I was an all-A student, queen of my middle and high school, and involved in every club known to man. I also earned the privilege to be named a school ambassador and the only freshman chosen to be a part of the varsity competition cheerleading squad. I participated on the dance line and even served as the basketball statistician one season. I set out to do it all. In the midst of all this, on a relational side, I was always a part of the cool kids crew. I only dated the popular guys, which most definitely came with its downfalls. There was only one guy during my time in Sandersville who I'm sure was aware of my true identity. He had known me since I was a little girl, and he was always so honorable. He was truly a great person. I was a rising sophomore when our relationship ended, and I had so much to learn about life. I decided that it would be smart to try a completely different type of guy for my next relationship. I had dated a really good guy, so why not try dating a cool dude, one that all the ladies loved and one who loved all the ladies. His name was Lance. He is one that you will hear much more about. I paid a heavy cost in tears, questions about my self-worth, and identity in this relationship. Lance and so many others knew the counterfeit Jackie I portrayed, and they were cool with her. The struggle between fitting in or just being true to myself was so real.

This struggle was even exemplified during my time at church. I can remember driving myself to my auntie's church when I became old enough. During worship I experienced a huge internal fight to stand up and lift my hands in worship, because nobody else my age was doing that. Of course I needed permission to lift my hands from all those around me, right? I had such a love for God, even then. Although I was in a counterfeit phase, the roots from which I was birthed were still deeply ingrained in me. Rather than introducing my friends to this girl who really loved God, I settled for people seeing me ride around with my top dropped, with the cool kids, the latest clothes, and my fake hair blowing in the wind as if this was all there was to me. Getting dressed up, going to the club, and watching people fight and act foolish was the highlight of some of our weekends. I have seen it all. Sandersville exposed me to the dude with the really good heart who pushed weight (sold drugs) as well as the valedictorian who wouldn't know weight to be anything other than the pounds of fat on his body. It allowed me to be friends with the single mother with multiple kids who was doing her best to make ends meet and the very sheltered young girl whose only care was if she was going to make the cheerleading squad. I had the broadest array of influences. I tell you, I was a mess trying to appease both audiences. One moment I was varsity-cheerleading-make-all-A's Jackie, and the moment I left school, I was superficial, knuck-if-you-buck Jackie, and everything in between. I was completely lost!

Have you ever been there? Is this your present life? Have you settled for a relationship, job, or way of living that doesn't reflect your true identity? Perhaps you made these decisions for the sake of not being alone, fitting in, or even due to some trauma of your past. My dad issues and early hair trauma played a huge part in shoving me into a life of covering the real me. It's crazy how life's happenings can cause us to cover or hide the very best part of ourselves. Rather than facing the breaches and keeping our eyes on the one who can truly heal, we go looking for a quick fix, and find ourselves with a thing that will only temporarily satisfy.

You see, the moment I was old enough to make my own decisions about my hair, I became a specialist in covering up one of the areas that was most vulnerable to me. I internally vowed that I would never give anybody else another opportunity to have an opinion about my hair. I could still hear the voices of my brother, cousins, and even friends at school making fun of my hair. I remembered being scarred so deeply by their looks and the whispered remarks. I wore hair extensions for as long as I can remember. It was a part of my new identity that I fully embraced so much that there were times when my mom would suggest me wearing my natural hair, and I would remark, "Yeah Mom, that's just not me!" Do you see how dangerous living in falsehood can be? **The counterfeit life will make you reject your truth if embraced for too long!** There were very few seasons where I wore my hair out, and it was always short-lived due to always feeling as if something was wrong with my hair. I felt naked without my additions. Even after my hair grew back and became healthy, I was still so damaged in this area.

Once you become comfortable with covers, conforming in other ways seems to always follow. Sandersville was the place where I gave away the most precious part of myself before marriage. It wasn't even because of my desire, rather it always came back to the same thing for me. I had a huge longing to always please everyone. This desire seems so superficial on the surface, but **I want you to know that there is always a deeper root that traces to the *why* behind our actions.** I wanted to please my parents, my teachers, my friends, and my boyfriends. You name it and I wanted to please them! As I reflect, I think this desire was deeply rooted in never wanting to feel rejected again, the way I did when my dad left. Because I didn't understand his absence, in my mind and heart it all became my fault. With my ignorance, I felt that I had to ensure I never gave anyone else a reason to leave. I thought if I did everything everyone wanted me to do, then surely they would stay and continue to "love" me.

It was clear that my daddy wound was still wide open. I can remember my brother and I standing outside in my grandma's yard seeing an airplane fly overhead and being sure it was our daddy coming back to be with us. For years, we jumped up and down every time we saw a plane. As we grew older, we recognized that he wasn't coming. I was in search of a father's love, one that secures and affirms your identity. When this place in my heart was left void, I allowed counterfeit love to fill it.

The people-pleasing and wanting permission also came as a result of a false sense of what love truly is. Somehow, in my mind, I believed that love equated to doing everything a person desired. I never wanted to disappoint anyone's expectation of me even if that meant losing the things I treasured or having to conform to engage in certain activities. With most of the silly choices I made during this time in my life, it all points back to trying to please someone else. **When you are no longer sure of your true identity, you begin to allow others' desires to dictate who you become.** As a result, my actions were often contrary to my true identity in Christ. I did whatever necessary to keep everyone satisfied with me or so I thought! What I found out is the more you try to please people, the more people-pleasing will be demanded. Humans are never satisfied. If you begin in a way where your whole objective is making sure every want a person has is satisfied, you'll get stuck in that cycle. They will continue to expect this of you, and their wish list never gets shorter. My mom had a saying that I should have listened to much sooner. She would say, "Jackie, you better start how you want to finish with people!" People believe whatever you demonstrate with your actions. I think lots of times we believe we can win a person by doing certain things, and then show them who we really are later. This is why it's so much better to be who we truly are from the beginning, so that we don't find ourselves imprisoned by the lie we initially presented.

I found this to be true in my relationship with Lance. I was lost when I entered the relationship, but somehow I believed he would recognize my real beauty and honor it. In retrospect it was somewhat unfair to expect that of him, when I didn't even honor myself. I stayed when he cheated, lied, and publicly embarrassed me. I taught him that his actions didn't have consequences and that I thought very little of myself. I was stuck on stupid. If you are here now, let me just pause to remind you that you have full permission to make a change.

There was a time, while living in counterfeit land, I think God knew I was desperate for change as well. I was so sick of living a basic life—one that was beneath who I really was and a life that majored in the superficial. The superficial seemed to be all that people cared about. We live in a world where we are measured by performance, wardrobe, who you date, and what you drive. I cried out many times to my mom during this counterfeit season because I knew she was clear about the real Jackie. She would often try to talk sense into me, but I was so deaf to truth, I couldn't even receive all the wisdom she was offering. To be honest, I don't think I even had the capacity to receive her advice for a lot of those years.

Then, God sent this woman to start a program at the church I was attending. This program was much different than anything I had ever been exposed to while in Sandersville. It was called *Princess Daughters*. Our Princess Mom would come down and impart into me and a few other young ladies at the church. She would remind us of our worth and how beautiful marriage is actually supposed to be. She led us through a vow of purity where we were able to rededicate our bodies back to the Lord and go forward in newness from that point. I was so excited because I was hearing language that spoke to a place so deep in me. I felt the real me who was hidden beneath all the layers trying to arise for the first time in so long!

This program was my way out and back to being the girl I was designed to be. I saw my boldness in Christ beginning to reemerge and I felt like my old self again. My Princess Mom was incredible. She carried herself with such grace and elegance, while at the same time she was a real down-to-earth woman. I admired the way that she loved God and how she always challenged us to be more than we currently were. This program was a Godsend. I only wish I had shut the door to all temptation and distraction before starting on this new road.

The thing that broke my heart about how the Princess Daughters situation ended is somehow I ended up back dating Mr. Lance. I felt that after all that I had gained from the few weeks of being in this program, I would be strong enough to stand my ground. I planned to reintroduce myself to this relationship from a whole place. It was all a fairytale. I held strong for a few months, but the relationship became what it had always been, all about what Lance wanted. It was with him where I went back on my vow of purity to God. It devastated me in a way I could never explain. Just when I was on the road to possibly finding my true self again, I plummeted even further down the wrong road than I had ever been. My Princess Mom could tell something was off with me, and she withdrew. I felt so disconnected emotionally every time we talked or hugged. It was as if she pulled her heart out of our relationship in an effort to shield herself from my demise. I think it was too hard for her to watch me live in a way that was not true to my identity. It wrecked me, so I gave up on the quest for new life too, until the summer before I left for college.

MIDNIGHT MILK RUN

I was so lost, and I'm not sure I was even aware of how far gone I was. There is one instance in particular that truly brings to life just how bad things were in the area of wanting to be loved and enduring absolutely anything to fill that void. One night my mom was working the night shift, and my brother, who was a senior at the time, rarely came home. He loved to stay with friends or family in town because we lived so far. Well, Lance and I decided that we wanted to spend some time together, so I went to pick him up. We were on our way back to my house, on the country roads that were very dark and full of deer at night. Lance decided that it would be funny to shut off the lights to my car and drive down these long, winding, deer-filled roads in the pitch black. To say that I became furious is an understatement. I'm sure there was much profanity and screaming in an effort to get this nut to turn the lights back on.

By the time we made it to my house, I was completely over even being near Lance. I left him out in the living room, went into my room, and began to clean. It was already late at this point, and I was so irritated. I kept asking him to let me take him back home. He refused to leave. As soon as I got my room exactly the way I wanted it, he came in and started to throw things off my dresser onto the floor. He knocked all the pillows off my bed and unmade my bed. At this point, the foolishness reached a level I could no longer tolerate, so I made him get his things so I could take him home.

By the time we were heading to his house, it was around midnight. I was so sleepy that I was having a hard time keeping my eyes open. We didn't utter one word to each other the whole twenty-five minutes to his house. Even as he got out of the car, it was completely silent. I got on the highway to head back home. The route that I took was undergoing construction except in one spot. I continued to doze off and wake back up the whole ride home. One time, I dozed off too long and woke up as I was bracing to hit one of the large orange construction cones.

I literally went off the road at the one area along this whole highway that didn't have the large boulders or cement blocks. My convertible Mustang flipped three times. It felt as if it was never going to end. I saw the roof opening above my head. When the car finally stopped, I was so grateful to be alive. It was freezing cold, and I was scared out of my mind. My mom had just bought me this car less than two weeks prior, and now it was destroyed. There was glass everywhere, and all hopes of finding my phone were shattered as I continued to hurt my hand on glass looking for it. I kicked the rest of the glass out of my driver's side window and climbed out. Because the area was so rural, the houses were very far apart. I began walking to find help due to there being no traffic on this road at that time of the morning. The first house where I arrived had a large "Beware of Dogs" sign as well as "No Trespassing!" I made the decision, in that moment, that it was way too dark to take any more chances. Having survived a wreck like that, there was no way I was risking being eaten by dogs.

The only option I had left was to continue walking until I got to another house. Talk about disappointed! It was time to begin walking again. As I was walking, I was sure that I was bleeding internally. I touched my ear and saw blood, so I automatically began thinking the worst. I was terrified, embarrassed, and full of shame. I tortured myself with words of how worthless I was and how dishonorable a daughter I must be to ever take my mom's trust and handle it this way. She gave her all for everything my brother and I were able to call our own. I was completely over myself.

When I finally arrived at the next house which was nowhere near the previous one, a couple came to the door. They were obviously alarmed due to how early in the morning it was. They welcomed me into their home and called an ambulance and the police. I was fully out of breath and crying uncontrollably. I was alive, but I wasn't sure that I was okay. The moment I was able to talk to my mom, everything got better. She got my Aunt Janise to come get me after the EMS workers confirmed that I was actually okay. I walked away from one of the worst car accidents ever with only a small scratch on my leg that bled a little. I must have touched that scratch before touching my ear, which made me think it was bleeding. Talk about the saving grace of the Father!

The best part of this story is the explanation I came up with to tell my mom why I was out driving so late to wreck my car. I told her that I was hungry and wanted cereal, so I drove to a store to get some milk. She actually believed me because I'm sure she didn't feel I had any reason to lie to her. She and I have always had a very close relationship, and I have always been honest with her. In this case, I didn't want to face the truth. I'm not sure what made me tell my awesome older brother the real story a few months later. I can remember him somewhat jokingly asking me, "Jackie, that night you had the wreck, what really happened?" Thinking I had been found out I played it cool initially, recounting to him the story I had told everyone else before. In the middle of this rendition, something made me feel that it was safe to tell Norman the whole story. This came after one hundred promises that he wouldn't say anything. Of course he broke that promise, and he went and spilled the news to my mom. It ended up being several months down the road before the whole truth came out between my mom and me.

When Norman told her, he made her promise him that she wouldn't come straight to me about it. She honored his wishes. The conversation with my mom about the truth kind of went the same way as it did with Norman. Something about the wreck came up and I felt this burden to tell my mom the truth. I asked her to promise me she wouldn't be mad at me, and she responded very well. All I remember her saying was that she couldn't believe I didn't feel that I could tell her the truth from the beginning. This made me feel horrible, and I promised her that I would never lie to her again.

The relationship with Lance definitely served me well. After this incident, he and I did continue dating off and on for some time, but things were never the same in my eyes. He soon left for college and his Casanova ways continued. Our relationship slowly continued to fizzle out over a long period of time. I experienced things and acted in ways I vowed to never do again. Sometimes hitting rock bottom is what it takes to recognize that you are worth too much to settle. For any young person reading this, I pray that you would believe the wise counsel around you and allow it to guide you. Please don't choose to learn the hard way and live through things like this to find yourself again!

In reflection, I am very grateful for the time I spent in Sandersville for many reasons. I was given liberties due to the small size of Sandersville that were presented to me way too early in life. In spite of this, God, in His sovereignty and grace, was able to make this time of my life still work for my good. I was able to maintain very high performance in the world of academia and extracurriculars, which equipped me well for college. From a personal perspective, I suffered many hard lessons that helped me tremendously in the long run.

Sandersville caused me to add a lot of fake layers that I would spend years undoing, but it also matured me beyond the foolishness of my youth. It showed me how very dangerous it is to live without having a firm grip on your true identity. It was also this location where I gained my present relatability and compassion for people of all kinds of backgrounds. My own errors and days of lost identity help me to see beneath the superficial stuff that intimidates most people. My previous pain enables me to see a person and understand that they too need someone to embrace and love them despite their mistakes. I have such a heart of grace and compassion for those who are struggling with grabbing a firm hold on their real identity, because I recognize firsthand how a person with a very good heart, even one that loves God, is capable of making decisions that do not in any way align with who they really are!

I tell people all the time who are struggling with shame from past decisions: **It is unfair to marry your real identity to the decisions you made when you had no idea who you really were! You must let the "counterfeit you" contend with those decisions, and recognize that the moment you choose to live your real life, you become free of the bondage of those past choices.** My mistakes may not be the same in amount or specific details to many that I meet, but I know, in God's eyes, whether one or a hundred, that we are all guilty the same. Sandersville demolished my ability to be judgmental, and it added so much effectiveness to the ministry God would call forth out of me in the next chapter of my life.

What I love most about my love story with God is even in this season He didn't second-guess His love for me. He watched over me and knew that the Jackie of Columbia existed even when I was too afraid to get to know her in entirety in Sandersville. Have you given up on yourself based on your present season, not recognizing that this season will change? You will grow and become all that God has for you. You have to get up and start your next chapter! This is the only way we continue forward!

Chapter Three

STATESBORO: I Woke Up

"Do not lie to each other, since you have taken off your old self with its practices and have put on the new self, which is being renewed in knowledge in the image of its Creator." —Colossians 3:9 NIV

I TOOK IT ALL OFF

The real me had been asleep for way too long. My Sandersville days were rapidly coming to a close, and I was looking at the new door of my life at Georgia Southern University. The summer before I left for school, I began to do a lot of reflecting. What I concluded was that the Jackie I presented in Sandersville did not leave me at a place of fulfillment as I prepared to close this chapter of my life. I was grateful for the many things I had gained! Wisdom, newfound perspective, and a huge desire to find my real identity again, to name a few. But the one thing that bothered me most was the idea of asking the people I was with every day if they knew how much I loved God, and them having no idea just how much He meant to me! This was heart shattering! I promised myself, in that moment, that I would no longer live the counterfeit life. I was ready to start this new chapter as the real me!

I arrived at Georgia Southern in August of 2006. My first weekend there, I was privileged to meet the friend circle I would carry with me for my entire college duration. What we came to call *The Square* was four friends who lived, slept, ate, and churched together. We were inseparable. *The Square* was comprised of Angie, Keshia, Camia, and myself—four girls from various backgrounds who were prepared to start this new journey of college together. We all came with our own set of baggage and things that would have to be changed along the way. One thing I can say is that we established, from the very beginning of this friend group, that God was always the main theme. I was seen as the "momma" of the group. By this time, I felt that I had experienced all the silliness life had to offer, and I was all about making good decisions that I would not look back and regret. I didn't do this perfectly. I still made silly choices from time to time. I was a college student, but it was clear based on my mind-set that I was heading in a much better direction.

My shedding process began. I decided that I would not pursue cheerleading, organizations, pageants, or anything of this nature. I wanted to experience what it felt like to just be Jackie with nothing added. I wanted to focus solely on academics and pursuing God. When I arrived at college, I wore hazel-colored contacts, if you can envision that. Wearing colored contacts was a very popular fashion trend at the time. As I was homing in on living my true identity without additions, it seemed as if everything that wasn't real began to bother me. I was finally able to see some of the things that many trusted voices in my life had been saying all along. I had an older cousin, Safarrah, who absolutely adored me when I was younger. He came home one Christmas, not long before I left for college, and said to me, "Baby, you don't need those contacts, take them out. They actually hide your beauty!" At the time, I thought to myself, "He just wants me to remain his little girl." I later realized that he actually saw the truth that I did not yet see.

I went through a process with my hair where I would go back and forth between micro braids and trying to wear my natural hair out. It was an up-and-down battle. There were times I found myself strong enough to face the vulnerability of having people make comments about my hair, and other times I was not so strong. My friend Angie was one of my greatest cheerleaders in this area. It's so crazy how damaged I was. I literally HATED if anyone made any kind of reference to my natural hair, be it good or bad. I automatically thought if they said something good, they were just trying to be nice because they could tell I was wounded. If they said something mean, it was a confirmation of what I already knew. The funny part is the enemy didn't stop there with his torment. If a person came around me and said nothing at all when my natural hair was out, then that was an insult as well. I made up in my mind all the things they were thinking in their head but were too polite to say. As you can see, there was no win during this time—just brokenness.

I realized something during the time of my hair battle. Although I removed the hair extensions and did the thing that I had been too afraid to do in my previous season, I hated the way I looked every day. When I looked in the mirror without my comfort blanket of hair extensions, I didn't even feel like myself. I found that you can know that you are living in a falsehood or doing something wrong, **but you will remain in bondage unless you pray and allow God to transform your mind about what you see or what you are doing.** You have to pray for real healing. **Doing things in your own strength is not freedom, it's behavior modification.** Behavior modifications don't have the power to bring about lasting change in our lives. The day I recognized that I was controlled by the world's view of beauty, I put my hair extensions back in and returned to my cover, knowing that I was not healed. I was happy that I was at least aware that God was still going to have to move in this area, and I began praying specifically for my mind to be renewed and for healing to take place in order to reach true freedom.

HE SET ME ON FIRE

I began attending an on-fire ministry in Statesboro, Georgia, known as *Spirit and Truth Worship Center*. This setting would provide the backdrop for me to embrace the radical nature of my worship for God and to begin the infantile stages of recognizing that I had a voice tailor-made for empowering. This ministry was filled with numerous college kids from a vast array of backgrounds and upbringing. What connected all of us was our love for Christ and a desire to live fully surrendered lives. For my friends and me, this ministry was such a huge part of our lives. We attended Sunday service, Bible study, nights of worship, events on campus, trips to other churches, and hermeneutics and homiletics classes. If the doors of that church opened, we were most likely going to be found in the number inside.

This was the first time in my life where I was exposed to other believers who loved God and pursued Him heavily in their youth. I became very close with two young ladies, Cassandra and Tarrah. I have to say that I was able to glean so much from both of them throughout my time at Georgia Southern. It was always clear that they both believed in the unique gift God had placed on my life, and they walked alongside me to help to uncover these gifts. Our leader, Pastor J, was the exact same way. I will forever honor this man for the deposit he made in my life. Pastor J always inspired me to just be me. He seemed to have such regard for the things God placed on my heart. He added me to a team of young people that he trained to be ministers and began to prepare me for my future, although I wasn't fully aware of it at the time. It had been prophesied to me that I would preach the gospel. I knew I had a unique call on my life, but I did not know how soon many of these things would manifest.

The thing I struggled with was the pressure to have to perform or speak a certain way because that's how the "spiritually elite" did it, rather than just be. I remember, as a result, I became somewhat stuffy for a season. I was more law-driven instead of resting in the great balance of God's grace and truth. I would often find myself engaging in judgmental conversations that reflected on the way people danced before the Lord or how their tongues sounded. It was obvious, I was having a season of the counterfeit again. Only now it was showing up in the spiritual arena. I began trying to live up to the expectations around me and fit in with the spiritually deep crew. It was all law and I was only able to exist this way for a short period. I began to feel I was losing sight of what Christianity was really about. I decided to go back to the drawing board so God could renew and teach me again what this life was really about, versus what people made living a spiritual life to be.

I can remember back to as early as my freshman year and throughout my time at Georgia Southern, how my friends and I would pursue God on our own. It was not uncommon for my friends (*the Square*) and I to convert our bedrooms or living room into a full-on church service. My friend Keshia is a very anointed prophetic dancer, Angie sings with such a yoke-breaking anointing, and Camia has such a sweet anointing for intercession. God often used me during these times to speak words of affirmation and to break down scripture to nourish us. We returned back to these basics many times, especially when we felt we were getting off course. We desired to serve God from a pure place. It was moments like these—where we sat before the Lord with no agenda, and times alone in my room crying out to God—that I truly established my own personal relationship with God. Having this personal relationship with the Lord is so fundamental to growing in our ownership of permission.

NERD JACKIE

As focused as I was on the purity of my spiritual life at Georgia Southern, I was just as focused on my dream of becoming a healthcare professional. I mentioned in the beginning of the book that my mom and dad were both pharmacists. I was also gifted to love math and science all my life, so pursuing a healthcare profession always made sense to me. I entered Georgia Southern majoring in Biology with the desire to become a dentist. I never wanted to become a pharmacist because I actually love interacting with people, and I didn't feel that there was enough interaction with people in that field. For as long as I can remember, I had always wanted to be a pediatrician. I ended up having a conversation with one of my hometown physicians before I left for school, and it changed my whole path. He knew that I was interested in healthcare. As we talked, he began to plant the seed that sparked this newfound desire to pursue dentistry. He had the whole plan laid out. He said I needed to go to school and major in Biology. From there, I would go on to dental school for four years and then apply for the specialty of Endodontics after I finished. Endodontists are the dentists who specialize in performing root canals. He said I would only have to work a few days a week. It would allow time for me to have a family and have a major impact in the lives of people. That sounded like a great plan, so I went fully toward it.

I was able to find a dentist who allowed me to shadow her, in an attempt to confirm that dentistry was the right profession for me. Dr. Eleonora Jenkins is one of the most phenomenal women I have ever met. She made dentistry look effortless and was very affirming about my path toward becoming a dentist. She serves as a lifelong mentor to me. I was so grateful God introduced me to this amazing woman, because she brought to life a plan that was just words at one time. I spent a whole summer shadowing her, and I was so excited about my future ahead as a result.

The course load at Georgia Southern was no joke. It took much diligence and hard work to matriculate in a way that would place me in good standing for admission into a dental school. This quest is where I became a little crazy while at Georgia Southern. After researching and listening to various advisors talk about all the things I needed to have in place, my perfectionism kicked into overdrive. It resurfaced on a whole new level. My freshman year, I was studious yet still much more like myself. I was very devoted, but not to a level of obsession. I made only one B, in general chemistry, during my time at Georgia Southern, the first semester of my freshman year. Our advisors made clear that withdrawing from classes was not optional. Withdrawals showed an application reviewer instability and lack of dedication. They ingrained in us that the higher your GPA, the better. There was not much room for error. B's were like F's to those who were looking toward professional school. I didn't know any of this my first semester. I was just relaxing and giving my best. Well, after many conversations like this and with the introduction of an amazing young lady named Yasmine Enmon, my study game and academic focus charted to territories unknown to many.

I became school-crazy. It looked good at the award nights, receiving honors for all A's and my 4.0 GPA for that semester. While there is nothing wrong with academic excellence, the problem came when I lost my peace. I was about to have a nervous breakdown at the thought of taking a test and not knowing the answer to *one* question. It didn't matter if there were a hundred questions, and I knew the answer to ninety-eight of them. I was going to obsess that whole night over why I got the two questions wrong. It was absolute madness. I literally recall one night being at Yasmine's house, and she was a worrywart of all worrywarts as well. It was already about 6:00 a.m., and we had to go in to take an organic chemistry exam at 8:00 a.m. We had already pulled an all-nighter trying to read about ten chapters which was humanly impossible anyway. We decided to just lie down and close our eyes for a couple of hours before the test. As we were lying there, Yasmine said, "Jackie, what if there is a question on the test about the one chapter of the ten we didn't get to?" We both jumped up with extreme fear, simply at the thought of missing one question. We stayed up the rest of the morning reading that chapter because missing one question was failure in our eyes. You may be reading this in full-fledged laughter, and you should be laughing. We were absolutely out of our minds. Our minds were so far gone that we didn't even know where to find them. To the people on the outside, Jackie and Yasmine were on top of everything and killing the game. It was more like the game was killing us.

ONE QUESTION CHANGED IT ALL

I remember calling my mom who is one of the most real women on this side of heaven. She doesn't know how to fake at all. I called her crying about how I was not prepared for a test and how I had so much anxiety. She literally said to me, "Bye Jackie! Call me back when you find my real daughter again!" I was a mess! I graduated with my Summa Cum Laude badge of honor, though. This is all that matters to society, right? I walked across the stage with my head held high because I matriculated through a four-year college while maintaining a 3.96 GPA. To the world, this accomplishment is the epitome of success. Dying in your private life trying to prove or achieve things others will be proud of is not truly living! I was doing all of this striving in my own strength; all while stamping Jesus' name on it as if He had led me to live this way. I have found that we are so confused about what success really is to God.

This story takes me back to a pivotal question God asked me one day while walking across the campus. School had just resumed after Christmas break, and I went back to school sporting several of my new outfits. I had a new boo, and I was killing it in the world of academia. I was looking good and feeling great about life. Amidst this, God stopped me in my tracks with a question. He said, "Jackie, what do you want to be known for?" I tried to respond with a quick remark. *God, I want people to know how much I love You!* God didn't say another word in that moment, but He disrupted my life in such a profound way with that question. This one question forced me into one of my deepest seasons of intimacy with the Father while at Georgia Southern. What I recognized is that I was again becoming content with losing my identity, this time to my performance in the classroom. Although

I remained focused in school, I expanded my eyes to see the importance of being identified as a woman of faith. They were all aware that I was a woman with a good GPA. You see—at the end of the day, if one of my friends was hurting or dealing with the loss of a loved one, there was nothing my good GPA could do for them. Knowing me as a woman of faith, however, would have had major impact. I could finally answer the question now. Yes, I wanted to be known as a carrier of Christ because it is the only identifier that has lasting effects. This decision brought about a huge shift in the way I did everything.

I began to allow God to sharpen my ear in this season. I asked His permission to do everything. *God, what do You want me to wear? Is it ok to go here? What do You want me to eat?* When I tell you nothing was off-limits, I mean nothing. He even began to transform the way I studied. I remember while enrolled in a Parasitology class asking God to show me how to write Him a love letter on this subject on my next test. I allowed Him to be the heartbeat of everything, even my study of parasites. I recall sitting in my room for hours, worshipping in the presence of the Lord. I offered Him everything. I even laid dentistry on the altar. I got to the point where I recognized that there was no job I was unwilling to do as long as it satisfied Him.

For admission into dental school there are so many requirements that you must fulfill. One of the biggest is the Dental Admission Test (DAT). I had all the requirements covered: outstanding GPA, shadowing hours, extracurricular activities, leadership skills, and even the extra things like research or internships that set you apart from the competition. All I had left was scoring well on my DAT, and acceptance should have been a shoo-in. Then, God threw a curveball. I took the DAT twice; I made a 14 and then a 15. I performed terribly, and I was devastated. The test is set on a scale of 30. I had always performed well on standardized tests, and the content covered all seemed pretty familiar. I just didn't understand. *Lord, why would You let me give this much energy toward a career in dentistry only to close the door with my DAT score?* I made the exact score that the reps had warned not even to apply with, because they wouldn't consider candidates with those scores.

It was like a horrible dream. Out of desperation I resolved to asking God, "Was this Your way of telling me that dentistry is not what You want for me?" I was truly open to His answer being that dentistry was not what He wanted. I did not submit my application until one day before the deadline because I had to be sure. I asked God to confirm that applying was His choice. The next day, I received a call from the main recruiter at the dental school I wanted to attend. She called to find out why she hadn't received my application. She told me to go ahead and submit my application (despite my DAT scores) and to see what happened.

I received a call some time later from this same recruiter, letting me know that I was invited to the Medical College of Georgia (MCG) in Augusta, Georgia, for a dental interview. I cannot even recount to you how excited I was and how much of a *God thing* I knew this had to be. MCG was the only dental school in the state of Georgia. Despite all of the recruiters' recommendations not to put all my eggs in one basket, it was the only dental school where I applied. It was now interview time!

Let me tell you—I know it was nobody but God who prepared me to have the type of poise and Godfidence that I carried into that dental school on the day of my interview. I stood shoulder-to-shoulder with the most elite students from all around the United States. God gave me a clear word. He told me that my future of becoming Dr. Jacqueline Gyamfi Greene was all up to Him. He let me know that if He decided that I would be accepted into dental school then there was nothing on this Earth that could stop that word from being established. These words were so necessary after the valley moment experienced after taking the DAT.

It was clear God orchestrated the whole interview process. I was interviewed by a pediatric dentist, Dr. Shafer, who happened to be best friends with her mom, the same as I was with mine. This connection made for easy conversation, and it was literally all we discussed.

I'm pretty sure my second interviewer was Dr. DeRossi. He is one of the biggest clowns you could ever meet. He made me feel right at home, so it was like talking with someone I had always known.

The most beautiful part of this day came when I encountered a girl having a full-on meltdown in the bathroom before her interview. It became clear that the words God used to give me courage weren't just for me. The girl became one of my classmates. She was from Georgia Tech. In the moment, I thought to myself, "I'm sure she blew the DAT out of the water, what reason does she have to be afraid?" God allowed me to pour the same words into her that He used to strengthen me. I recognized that it didn't matter how well you could perform. Performance in your own strength can only take you so far. Eventually, you will fail yourself and find that you are in need of a Savior who has the ability to sustain you. God used my poor performance on the DAT to strip me of the confidence I had in myself. He wanted me to begin this journey of dentistry the right way. I knew that it would have to be God to grant me admission into this school, therefore only He could sustain me through the entire process. He tied my hands! He didn't want me trusting in my own strength, and that's exactly what I would have done had I gotten in by my own merit.

Just a short time after my interview, I received the call to inform me that I was selected to be one of seventy students to comprise the 2010 dental class at the Medical College of Georgia! Through this trial and so many of my other failures and proclivities, God exposed me to a love that I had never known. It is a love that is so consistent and relentless. I recognized that despite all my imperfections, I am still God's choice. Even in the moments where I failed, He somehow still made ways for me. This is also true for the areas in your life where you have missed the mark. In spite of us, God is so faithful to perform on our behalf. There is nothing we can do to separate ourselves from His unconditional love. It was at this moment that I made the choice to serve God with all of me. God established Himself as not just the God of my mom and grandma. He became *my* God, one who I grew to affectionately refer to as Daddy.

My struggles with my earthly father were still present. Being that he and Mom divorced when I was young, and he lived so far away, I went many years without seeing him. From year four to year twelve, to be exact. He called on our birthdays and holidays and we knew we could reach out to him if needed, but due to the lack of time together, I still faced many struggles. At the recommendation of my mom, I reached out to my dad to try to explain the effects that his absence had on me. I told him how I felt like if I were perfect, he never would have left. That having my mom love me so hard and know every detail of my life, weighed against a dad who I wasn't sure even knew my favorite color, made the void even bigger.

He was very apologetic and eager to do anything to help. I told him that I desired for him to be more intentional about getting to know me. He began to call more regularly, and it was so weird. I didn't recognize, until this happened, that the void I thought my dad still needed to fill, was actually a God-sized void that could only be filled by God. This allowed me to finally come to peace with my dad being in Africa and loving me from there. I was so grateful to have this newfound wholeness. This opened the door to a very healthy relationship between my father and me. I had to allow God to do the heart work that my dad, in his best efforts, could never do. God healed me!

We have situations in our lives that may have had specific characters involved. These life happenings could have been pain and bruises we carried for years. What I recognized through the situation with my dad is that although he was a character in the story of me battling with rejection, he is not a healer! Only God can step into these deep, private, tucked-away occurrences and heal us. This healing that was needed in my heart was not on my dad. I had to seek the God who heals in order to be restored back in this area of breach. What I love is that once I reached this place of wholeness with God, peace with my father immediately came. Maybe you are still battling with something, and feel that if you could just be healed of this one thing, you could regain your rightful image of yourself and live in the permission God has granted you. If that's you, I pray in this moment that you will pause and recognize God as healer, and allow Him to come in to free you for real!

WHEN GOOD ISN'T GOOD ENOUGH

I dated the same guy off and on for most of my undergrad career at Georgia Southern. For the sake of this book, let's call him Matt. Matt and I met in the spring of my freshman year. When Matt arrived on the scene, one of the most unforgettable things happened. The day I met Matt, I saved his number in my phone as "God Sent Friend." Matt was a really cool guy. We were very good friends. We ultimately took things forward to a full-on relationship not long after we started hanging out. I often look back and wonder if it was ever supposed to be that way. Don't get me wrong. Matt was a really good boyfriend. He wasn't perfect, but I would overwhelmingly say he loved me with his best knowledge of *love* at the time. The reason I question if he was ever supposed to become my guy is the timing in which he entered my life. I was in devoted pursuit of going deeper with God, and Matt made me very comfortable. He wasn't a bad guy, but he didn't challenge me to live above the place I already existed in God. All of the challenges came from me. The desire to live pure came from me. The desire to go deeper in God came from me. Matt was fully satisfied with a comfortable Jackie, so I already knew that he would not be the kind of guy who could lead me in my future.

You see, I had to make Matt go to class. I would talk to him about the importance of being a part of a church. He was okay with the status quo, and that was in total opposition of who I was designed to be. I dealt with a lot of internal turmoil concerning Matt. Matt came from a great family. He grew up in a two-parent household. He had an amazing mom, dad, and granny who I grew to love dearly. There was nothing wrong with Matt when looking at our relationship from the outside, based on the world's standards. The world told me over and over again that my standards were just too high. According to them, I shouldn't have had an expectation for a man to honor my purity, be faithful always, or lead me spiritually. This is the prevailing "truth" of our world today. For a long time, I went to church without Matt and grew deeper in my relationship with God. I struggled with releasing Matt to be ready for the woman for whom he was actually designed, versus continuing to hold on because of embracing the lie that my standards were too high.

I wrestled many times, while standing at the altar at church, "God, if I leave his life how will he ever get to know You better? How will he ever reach the full potential for his life?" Because you all missed the fact that I was his Lord and Savior Jackie Gyamfi, right?! So I would go through seasons of walking away and somehow settling right back into a life of comfort with Mr. Matt. I had been willing to lay so many things down at God's feet. With my hands held high in surrender, I kept one hand closed clutching this one thing—my relationship with Matt. It was safe. It was easy. It was a good relationship according to worldly standards. I mean, heck! It was at least better than the relationship I had with Lance back in Sandersville. We are supposed to settle for good as long as it's better than what we experienced before, right? I'm so grateful I had an aunt who never relented in telling me I wasn't crazy for feeling that Matt wasn't it. She went further to affirm the fact that God placed the desires that were deep within my heart, and that He would fulfill them. She was basically saying again, "Baby, live your truth! You have full permission to obey that desire deep within you, given by God."

Can I just free some man or woman reading this book to go and live your truth as well? I have found that the enemy of Great is Good. You will often have to give up what is Good in one season in order to receive that thing which is perfectly made for you—your Great thing in the next. I want to be clear—there was absolutely nothing wrong with Matt. He has now gone on to become happily married with a baby girl and all. He just wasn't my husband. I think he was always supposed to be a good friend, but I tried to make him something God never designed him to be. That's a word for my ladies right there! There was a Great man that God handcrafted with me in mind, and I believe this holds true for you, too. God uniquely designs relationships, jobs, and even friendships to help facilitate our journey of becoming. We have to be content with releasing Good to receive what God has designed to be Great for our lives.

TRAVIS MEETS KATHY

They say the counterfeit will often show up before the real thing. How crazy is it that I met Matt one semester prior to being introduced to the man who would become my husband. He is my Great thing! It was the fall of 2007 around October, and God sent a guy by the name of Travis Greene back to his alma mater to sing at an event called *Inspiration*, sponsored by the church I attended, *Spirit and Truth!* Travis graduated Georgia Southern in May of 2006, right before I was getting ready to enter.

He had two sisters, who I love to pieces, still attending *Spirit and Truth* with me. I had no idea they had a brother until this night at *Inspiration.* It was very unique to me that, although I didn't know him, I recognized his face. I had seen this face one other time prior in the student union at Georgia Southern. This place was where everybody gathered for lunch and to socialize. For those of you who know me, you know that it was very rare for a guy, even during my single days, to catch my eye. I recalled seeing this face. He was sitting on the stage in the union as I ate my lunch with friends at the balcony of Chick-fil-A. I asked one of my friends if she knew him. She didn't so that was the end of the story. I never thought about it again until I saw this familiar face the night of *Inspiration.*

Travis's plan was to come to *Inspiration* and sing a little of his first single, "Still Here." What transpired was something totally different, and I was absolutely floored. God had given Travis specific instructions, as he got up to take the stage, to declare everything God told him to say instead of singing. The crazy part is this campus was Travis's old stomping grounds. He was known as a Kappa man, and all the ladies loved him. He counted his reputation as nothing, and it had to be one of the greatest revivals that campus has ever seen. He began to prophetically speak about how there were groups of people struggling with fornication, depression, homosexuality, suicide—all things that run rampant on college campuses. He would announce a stronghold and instruct those individuals who were struggling with it to go to a particular area. He proceeded to then go lay hands on people and pray until they were set free. I was among the people who helped him pray and deliver others, as well as one on the receiving end of prayer. It was one of the craziest nights of my life.

I had never encountered a man that young demonstrating the power of God at that level. I was blown away by his commitment to obey God above his own agenda. I loved how radical and unapologetic his love for God was. He alluded to his previous reputation being that of a frat boy who ran the yard, but to watch his passion for seeing the lives of his peers set free, you could tell that the previous reputation meant nothing to him. He laid it down with ease for a much greater call. He was on fire and I loved it! His worship, smile, and his personality were all captivating. I had never encountered a person like him before. All my life, I only had one request as it pertained to the type of man I would marry. I know many women have a very long list. My list only held this one thing: I wanted my husband to love God the way I love Him. I know that I have a very genuine love for God which produces radical faith. I knew that my husband would have to speak this same language in order for us to even understand each other.

That night, as we were leaving *Inspiration* and heading home, my friends and I were in the parking lot, and we heard a guy ask, "Hey, what's y'all's name?" All of my friends said their names, and I ended by saying my name is Jackie. Travis, in return said, "Oh, alright Kathy!" I responded with a little attitude, "Kathy?! My name is Jackie!" He said again, "Oh, alright Kathy!" This little game was supposed to be his way of flirting. I found out, sometime later, Travis had a rule to never get a girl's number the first time he met her, even if he liked her. He was as cocky as he wanted to be. He said if it was meant to be, he would see her again. Even with his cockiness, I guess he was right.

About a month later, my church put on a night of worship event, and Travis was invited to come again. My church was actually where he got his start as a worship leader, when he was in college, so this was like coming back home for him. The whole night, as Travis played the keyboard, he eyed me in the audience. As he lifted up songs of worship to the Lord, he was skilled enough to flirt with me, all at the same time. Well I tell you, those big pretty brown eyes created one of the weakest spots in my heart for him. We ended up standing beside each other, in this back area of the church, along with lots of mutual friends. Remember, I had only met this crazy guy one time, one month prior in the parking lot. This guy started by announcing to all the people standing in the back, "Hey guys! I'm going to marry me a *Spirit and Truth* woman," while looking right at me! Again, this was the name of this church I now attended. After making this declaration, in good ol' Travis fashion, he took my phone out of my hand, and called himself from it. He handed it back to me remarking, "See, you didn't even have to ask for my number!" When I tell you this young man was bold, I mean it!

The connection between Travis and me didn't stop manifesting itself there. As my friends and I were heading home, my phone rang. Travis asked, "What are you all about to do?" I responded, "Go home!" It was around 2:00 in the morning when our night of worship ended. He asked, "Do you and your friends want to come to Waffle House?" I asked my friends, and they were cool with it, so we went. I must say I was a bit excited to get to know this guy a little more.

When we arrived at Waffle House, I sat by Travis. We held hands and communicated as if we had known each other forever. Well I tell you, all of this was out of character for me. I was tough, but everything felt so natural with Travis. We even witnessed to our waitress that night, and I started taking her to church with me. Her name was Jennifer. She was so sweet.

This was the beginning of our love story. He was like no man I had ever met. We had five- to six-hour-long phone conversations. He lived in Warner Robins, Georgia, at the time, where he was establishing life after college. We shared the deepest, most intimate parts about ourselves, and we fully embraced each other. He was a true man of God—one whom I would not even kiss for the first three years. We had the same values, morals, and ambitions. He was an absolute breath of fresh air.

Everything started out so wonderfully, but we most definitely had several bumps in the road along the way. Travis was still very young and had plenty of maturing to do, in terms of getting over himself. He said that I was the first girl to challenge him, have my own opinion, and not just go for whatever he felt like dishing out. We never argued in our times of dating. It was a cycle of getting all the way in there, one of us saying something the other didn't like, and both deciding we were not calling back. We would then go months without speaking until he popped back up in Statesboro, and the saga began all over again!

During the time of being introduced to Travis, Matt had been forced to leave Georgia Southern and return home due to not performing well in his classes the previous semester. His departure resulted in an off-season for us. As I progressed through my time at Georgia Southern, Matt was able to return. We had our bouts of being off and on as I spoke about earlier. Mr. Greene popped in from time to time to make sure he still had his place in my heart, but most of my time at Southern was with Matt.

All of this changed my senior year. It was the era when I started looking seriously at my journey ahead. I determined, in my heart, that I had to finally end things completely with Matt. Travis was nowhere in the picture at this time. I came to grips with the fact that I had seen several women struggle with having to lead their household, even with a husband. Many chose to live this way because they loved to be in control. I witnessed divorce after divorce, and I decided I didn't want this kind of life. I knew, in the world's eye, the women who were independent and chose not to submit were regarded as bosses. But I saw the weight of them playing the role of men when they had been created to be women. Men were created to lead. The reality hit me that this was what I would be signing up for if I continued forward long-term with Mr. Good, I mean Matt. What I loved was that Matt was fully aware of the chasm between us. One of the last times I saw him, he told me that he wanted me to be happy. He wished me well as we finally broke things off for the last time. He told me to go ahead and marry one of those suit-wearing church guys. He was right that my husband would be a man of God, but Travis rarely steps out in a suit!

Although I knew there was something very special about our relationship, I had come to the place of questioning if Travis and I would ever have a future together. I knew Travis loved Jesus, and even that he had feelings for me. I also recognized that he hadn't made the decision to give me his heart fully, and I wasn't willing to be an option even for a GREAT guy. I was at peace my senior year with dating God and allowing Him to bring whatever man He saw fit to lead me in my future.

In March of my senior year, not long before graduation, Travis reemerged in a way that was much more serious than before. I love to tell people that he was on his third strike. He even overcame his name being saved in my phone as *Never Again*! This was not the way I saved his number initially. Somewhere throughout the journey of him taking me on up-and-down emotional roller coasters, being at the altar one day and too full of himself to call the next, I was over it. I changed his number to Never Again, only to still answer after his second attempt at calling. I held strong for several months and began to move forward with my life, but he always knew how to weasel his way back in. This young man had created such a soft place in my heart for him.

I am the one to tell you that God is able to work miracles, believe me. Travis came back playing no games. It was the Pastor's Anniversary weekend at *Spirit and Truth*, and he wanted everybody to know that I was his girl. Due to his player-boy days at Georgia Southern, he had a way, in the past, of flirting with me without letting everybody (especially certain people) at the church know we were talking. Many people, just based on the little that they did see, had many things to say about me trusting Travis with my heart. They had been present when he was frat-boy Kappa Travis, and you know people don't let go of the past easily. All of this was neither here nor there at that point, because he was back and wanted everybody to know about us.

The faces of utter astonishment when we left or sat together at the church were absolutely hilarious. Only our close friends knew about this long love history that had been brewing since back in '07. We had a blast with it. I was fine being his girl at this point because I could tell he was now ready. He only had one more silly moment after we went steady in March.

After having an amazing weekend while he was in Statesboro, he got back home and told me that he had to be honest with me. He prided himself on the fact that he had never lied to me. He said that there were two other girls who he had been dating, and he wasn't sure which of us he was supposed to choose. Y'all, I wasn't even mad at Travis after this call, because I was so secure in who I was as it pertained to my worth. I told him, very emphatically, that he need not call my phone until he got that figured out. I knew that I was too valuable for this type of foolishness. I knew my husband would know that I was his only option! I don't think it even took Travis the full day to get his mind right. He called back to inform me that he had completely closed all other doors. He said he realized I was the only person he would never want to live without. We were full steam ahead from that point forward. My graduation day came. For my celebration, Travis penned a song called "One Ring Away!" Go to YouTube to hear the lyrics. He sang it to me again the night of our engagement. It was clear: I was the future Mrs. Greene, and now I was on my way to dental school.

Chapter Four

AUGUSTA: Stepping into the New

"And we know that for those who love God all things work together for good, for those who are called according to his purpose." —Romans 8:28 ESV

HE BROKE ME TO REBUILD ME

Dental school was a place of major breaking for me. I thought in my previous season in Statesboro, God required me to totally lose confidence in myself. I had no idea what this actually meant until I began dental school. From the start of dental school, everyone had so much excitement, simply for being accepted into such a rigorous program. We had no idea, what we were really in for. Our excitement quickly transformed into questions. Many of my peers and I wondered if we made the right choice with our future as we were exposed to so many new skills that we were expected to master all at once. I tell people who are interested in dentistry all the time: It's not that dental school is hard as much as it is a very hard adjustment! You have to adjust to a workload that is almost ten times the amount you were exposed to in undergrad. You have to adjust to coming from a world where you are the absolute best at everything to having a few things that may take some practice to master. Things such as waxing teeth and doing crown preps. You have to adjust to not making A's on everything. It's an entirely new way of life. I feel that the persistence needed to navigate this phase of my journey set me up to recognize that all I had been called to would be unattainable, unless I was sure and committed to the task at hand.

It is no different than those of you who have ventured into new jobs, stepped out to be entrepreneurs, or have become new parents. We all come to a place where we realize that the learning curve is real. I don't know about you, but some of the toughest seasons of my life have been when I was amidst the learning-curve process. To make matters worse, dentistry is the mixture of art and science. It is both subjective and objective, which makes mastery even more difficult. Due to being a recovering perfectionist, my first year of dental school completely destroyed my flesh. Although the grip of societal success had loosened some, it was something I still fought with in my early days of dental school. I can't tell you the number of conversations Travis and my mom endured as I fought to kill this perfectionist nature in me. I would ask them so many questions because I didn't know how to do it on my own. Have you ever felt that you knew God was trying to take you to another level, and the space between you knowing this and living it was excruciating? That is exactly where I was.

I remember coming home after tests, practicals, and even some days after sitting in lectures feeling so overwhelmed. I wanted to be in control of all of it, and I was not. I desired to get a grip on this new phase of life, and I wasn't even close. I prayed and cried and cried and prayed all up until the point that I finally gave up. I gave up trying to do it my way, and I finally arrived at the place where I was open to hear God's perspective on where I was. He helped me to be willing to do it another way.

I began asking God questions that helped progress me through the space of knowing He wanted me to live new, and actually living new.

One day I said, "Ok God, so what is success?" He said, "**Success is living a life of obedience to Me.**" I found a verse that totally backs this up and I began to meditate on it. In Proverbs 12:14 it says there is a way that seems right to a man, but its end is the way to death. What I saw from this scripture was that I can have an entire plan mapped out in my mind. I can even think it's right for my life, and be totally headed toward death and not life. This scripture means that the only way to live a successful life is to do that which you have been instructed by the Father to do. First Kings 2:3 also talks about how walking in obedience to God will cause you to prosper in all you do. I recognized that living a successful life was more equivalent to obedience than it was to titles, levels of income, or a grade I acquired. I began to gain freedom. I stopped striving for a thing and began striving to obey at all cost.

This didn't totally erase my old ways of thinking, and so there were moments that I even tried using God's Word on Him. I asked God, "I thought Your Word said that I am the head and not the tail and come above and not beneath." I had always equated this to mean that it was a mandate from God to always perform in excellence in all that I did. God said back to me, "Baby, all these things are true, but what is excellence?" I have come to gather, as I have walked with God, that excellence has much more to do with giving your all to a thing rather than a specific outcome. God wanted me to be fully devoted to all that He called me to and to give my best effort according to the gifts and talents He had given to me.

Being the head and not the tail did not mean that I would make an A every time, but it did mean that I would walk in Godly success and excellence. Doing things His way would establish me far above my efforts to try and produce a specific outcome. I turned, at this point in my life, from a person who was satisfied by making A's to a person who was satisfied by fully obeying God. God continued to give me instructions to strengthen me in this area. It was this newfound understanding that would be one of the most profound cornerstones for my new freedom in Christ.

Dental school was spiritual boot camp for me. During my preparation for exams, God tested my ability to obey Him. Knowing my previous history with trying to cross every T and dot every I, God forced me to trust Him. Several times when I had only partially reviewed all the material, God would instruct me to close all my notes and go ahead and go to sleep. He would say, "I'm going to show you if you lean in on Me, how much I will allow you to recall just from sitting in lecture." The demand for trust and obedience didn't stop there. On the way to my test the next morning, while riding in my car, God instructed me not to miss anyone on my way in to lecture who may be in need of a hug, smile, or whatever He needed for me to provide to them. Let me make this picture clear. While all my other classmates were fully engaged in their last-minute cram session, God had me out being an obedient servant to Him. He would not even let me open my notes once I made it to my seat.

If this wasn't hard enough, after taking the test, God would no longer allow me to go home and review my notes to try and figure out the ones I got right or wrong. He would ask, "Jackie, did you give your best?" I would say, "I obeyed You, Lord." He would say, "Well, you gave your best!" The way He made me even stronger with not equating an outcome with success was unbelievable. God wouldn't allow me to look at my grades for several days to weeks after they were posted. My whole class would receive an email from one of our professors, saying the grades from our previous exam were posted. God would say, "Jackie, don't go look!" While commotion filled the classroom and many people displayed various emotions, God was requiring me to understand that my success or failure was not found in a letter grade. It was found in the ability or lack thereof to trust and obey God.

I lived a very peculiar dental life. After grabbing ahold of the countercultural revelations God instilled in me, many of my past struggles became obsolete. The story of my life in dental school was that of trust and obedience. I wasn't known as an honor student in dental school although I graduated with a 3.7 GPA. The one thing people knew for sure was that I was a woman of faith. Many think that choosing to give control to God will somehow result in becoming a failure, which is the furthest thing from the truth. I still did very well in school, but I did even better by God. I grew leaps and bounds spiritually while there, and I gained a freedom that was life for me.

I attended a dental Bible study throughout my years at MCG, and I became closest with these girls during my time in school. We all understood each other's struggles, so we cried together, vented, prayed for one another, and learned more about how to live out this Christian life while matriculating through dental school. I grew to love Lindsey, Leann, Trisha, Jessica, and Devon, just to name a few, as if they were my own family. We studied things like *Follow Me* by David Platt. We read *The Story* by Zondervan. I would recommend that anyone who is looking to go deeper with God should read or watch either of these studies. They both had a huge impact in my life.

CIRCLE OF LOVE

I was honored to marry the love of my life, during Christmas break of my sophomore year. Travis was living in Mooresville, North Carolina, at the time, working at an amazing ministry in the South Park area of Charlotte. Our union only pushed me further in the direction of true freedom. Our wedding was an all-out affair. We had a bridal party of twenty-six people. Over two hundred and fifty people attended. It was the celebration of a true love. Our theme was *The Circle of Love*, which was one of the most beautiful things about our wedding, in my opinion. It was so surreal to me that God allowed Travis and me to be a continuation of his mother and father's beautiful love story. Due to the unexpected passing of Travis's father at the age of twenty-eight caused by an aneurysm, his mother was left to raise him and his two sisters, Kim and Shalonda, as a single mother. She never remarried. Travis was handed down his father's wedding band, to serve as a symbol of his heavenly covenant we were entering into. The circle of their love continued through our new bond.

It was such a gorgeous day. The air was filled with so much love and the Spirit of the Lord. Floating candles in tall glass vases surrounded Travis and me at the altar. We stood in a bed of red rose petals with a host of rich-colored live floral arrangements, all throughout. My dad was able to be a part of the wedding, and he alongside my mom spared no expense, to ensure that this day would be a moment I would never forget. It was everything I dreamed of and more. We wrote custom vows from our hearts, and they ended up being a major topic of conversation following our ceremony. The reception was in keeping with the same elegance and beauty. God's presence was so rich that whole day. It was the start of a new life with a man whom I still cherish and adore. The highlight video of this dream day is also on the Internet. Go look it up to allow this imagery to become reality!

Due to still being in school, the next two years we maintained a very healthy marriage long-distance. We were so grateful for God's grace not only on our wedding day, but to sustain our marriage through this unique time period. We created a schedule where a certain number of days he stayed in Augusta with me through the week, and on the weekends I drove up to North Carolina to be with him. This was amidst all the rigorous demands of dental school. I was so grateful for my newfound freedom, because it aided me in stepping into this new season well. God is so strategic to have you undergo parts of your process just in time to be prepared for the steps He sees ahead.

SIXTY-THREE DAYS IN BED

At the point where treating patients became our predominant task in dental school, it was clear that God was fast-tracking me. There was a large number of procedural requirements that we had to fulfill on patients in order to graduate. I was able to see that God had given me a special grace with people. I could literally recommend any treatment I deemed necessary for my patients, and they would accept it. They always showed up for their appointments and even filled the few cancellation spots I did have without a thought. All of this helped to place me as the first person in my class to fulfill all my requirements. The crazy part is that it was almost six months before graduation.

We found out we were pregnant with our very first child during my senior year of dental school. To say we were excited would definitely be an understatement. In my twentieth week of pregnancy, I went in for my anatomy scan. We had planned to receive the paper with the gender of the baby in preparation for our gender reveal that weekend. During my anatomy scan, it was clear that something was very wrong. The sonographer wasn't able to give me any information. When my OB came into the room, she was totally out of it. I called her by her name and asked what was going on. She instructed me to call my mom and tell her to get back to the hospital. My cervix was wide open which allowed my amniotic bag to bulge down through the opening. Due to the condition being so severe I was immediately admitted into the hospital. These findings were all to my surprise. I had just finished seeing patients, and this visit was supposed to be a quick stop before I headed to the chiropractor.

The answer to a question I had been asking since I entered into the clinical portion of dental school was beginning to unfold right before my eyes, and I had no idea. I would often say, "I wonder why God is so strategically fast-tracking me in completing all of my dental requirements so rapidly?" I was, unknowingly, at the entrance of one of the greatest storms of my life to date. I want to share with you something my husband often says that encouraged me even in that moment! He says, "**God has a plan before we have a problem! He has a solution before we ever have a situation**!" All of this proved to be true in my life. The fact that God is Alpha and Omega was made more real through this journey than ever before.

I remember the staff forcing me to be transported to my room via wheelchair. At this point, it was becoming clear that my current condition was extremely severe. This was my first baby! I thought to myself, "Lord, what is happening?!" We made it to my room, and I asked the nurse, "So I know the doctor said I had to be admitted, but do you know how long I will be here? Will this be a few days or weeks?" She was so gracious when she responded. She said, "You may want your family to bring you all the things you love to pass time! You could be in here for several weeks!" Talk about being hit with the unexpected. I was still so optimistic at this time. That night, we decided to go ahead and open the envelope that held the gender of our baby. We were pregnant with a baby boy who we had already decided to name David Jace Greene. David, because this is one of Travis's favorite Bible characters, and he has several impactful mentors with this name. Jace was the name of one of my dental school friend's son. When I found out its meaning, I was sold. Jace means *Healer* and *the Lord is my salvation*. We were in for the fight of our lives.

They had a high-risk obstetrician come in to talk things over with my family. She spoke regarding the prognosis and our options depending on the way things progressed. She was a Godsend. We were at the point where I had the option to undergo a procedure known as a cerclage. This procedure closes the cervix and helps provide support by placing a stitch that will keep the cervix closed for the duration of the pregnancy. It is best when this procedure is done preemptively. In my case, where my amniotic bag was already bulging down through the opening of my cervix, we were told that my son would only have a fifty percent chance of survival if we opted to do the procedure. Being able to manipulate the bag back up through the cervical opening and get a stitch in place without rupturing the bag was going to take a miracle of God. The flip side was if we decided to do nothing, it would be much more likely for my water to break and decrease the likelihood of our child's survival.

We all came together to pray and decide what we felt God was leading us to do. I pray that you are truly grasping the reality of where we were as parents. I went in for a doctor's appointment expecting to receive the envelope for my gender reveal. Instead, I was lying in a hospital bed being told that they would put me to sleep to do a procedure, and I could only hope my child would still be alive when I woke up. Talk about moments of desperation. We decided, after praying, that we felt peace about moving forward with the procedure.

Before they wheeled me back to the operating room, my family surrounded my bed including the high-risk OB who would be performing the procedure. I recall seeing her weep as my family prayed down the manifested presence of God. We were sure that our baby boy was in God's hands, and that there was no safer place he could be! We gave God our complete trust. I went into surgery and awakened to the news that, although it was a tough procedure, they were able to complete it successfully! My baby boy was doing great, and I was so grateful!

I was confident that the worst was behind us. Although I knew I would have to be very careful until time for delivery, it was great to know that Jace was out of immediate danger. They let me go home at the end of that week with orders of strict bed rest. I went back in the next Monday for a checkup. When I returned, they saw that my bag was bulging down around the stitch. They told me it would now be necessary to remain in the hospital for the duration of my pregnancy. The next day, in the wee hours of the night, as Travis and I were sitting up talking, I began to feel fluid start to leak. I immediately began saying, "Travis, there is no way my water just broke!" Remember we had already been told how horrible this could be. I was only twenty-one weeks at the time.

It was indeed my water, so we laid there the rest of the night waiting to hear what my regular OB would say when she arrived the next morning. The next day, she pulled Travis into the hallway and told him, "It's obvious that your son isn't going to make it! You all should just allow me to take the baby out and go home and try again." "Go home and try again" is what you say about a race or test you can easily redo. She was talking about the life of our son! We informed her that our high-risk OB had already told us that even if my water broke, we had the option to continue to fight and just see how things went. We declared that we trust God too much to give up. We were committed to continuing to fight no matter how bad the situation looked in the moment.

The outpouring of love and support we received during my hospital stay was out of this world. Phone calls, text messages, hospital visits, cards, edible arrangements, and care boxes literally filled my room. The way God showered us with love during this time was so beautiful. My aunt/cousin Lavern came one day and declared, in spite of knowing all that had transpired, that God said, "Jackie shall have a healthy baby boy!" It was declarations like this, Bible devotionals, lots of prayer, and support that helped carry me through. My mom stayed by my side every night despite having to leave each day and go directly to work. Many of my family members and friends came to visit. My in-laws were right there every step of the way, praying and checking on us. One of my aunts even pulled away from home to come and sit with me and encourage me through this tough time. Several people from my dental class along with other friends and family began this weekly celebration. They began to wear colorful bands around their wrists, and each week that we made it without Jace coming, we removed another band. This was our way of celebrating the fact that God had held him another seven days. We even had several nurses participate in this celebration. God blessed me to be cared for by some of the most phenomenal nurses ever.

In the life of a premature baby, being able to gain another week of gestation could be the difference between suffering major health issues or not. Each week was a miracle to us. Our goal was twenty-six to twenty-eight weeks gestation, at the minimum. We were told Jace would have fully developed lungs and his viability would be more concrete at this point. I was placed on magnesium sulfate treatments to try and limit my contractions during this process. Those treatments were very severe. They caused extreme weakness, headaches, and just an overall terrible feeling. I can remember Travis's face every time they said they had to start another one of those treatments. It was full of so much compassion. He felt so bad that I had to endure this.

Each day, sonographers would come around to let me know how much amniotic fluid I had left. This was a very hard part of the journey. I was aware that this was the fluid that supplied nourishment to our baby. The more he lost, the more critical our situation became. I got down to 1.45 cm and critical level was anything below 2 cm. I felt so low the day my levels dropped below critical. I began to pray because I had been lying in this same hospital bed for several weeks. I was only twenty-six years old, and I was watching my legs begin to wither due to inactivity. I had to brush my teeth out of a cup and bathe in bed as well. Each time I had to use the restroom, I had to prepare to fight with IV cords hooked to every part of me, just to get to my bedside toilet. I began pleading with God to somehow perform a miracle.

My husband went to my mom's house one day during this desperate time, to shower and rest a while. He had no idea that God was going to give him a prophetic declaration through song that helped encourage us as we persisted in faith. We were at our lowest. We knew all the facts my regular OB presented. We knew that several nurses had been told not to give us false hope because it was very likely our situation wouldn't end favorably. Despite all of these opinions, God gave Travis these words, and he called to sing them over me! This song came, not after we were through the fight, but right in the middle of it. We said even with our faith weak: *Lord, You made a way, when our backs are against the wall and it looked as if it is over. Lord, You made a way, and we're standing here only because You made a way.* We had no idea how this song would take the world by storm and become the major anthem for many around the world facing hopeless and dire situations!

We began to see the words to this song manifest. On Easter Sunday, the sonographer came around to let me know what my fluid levels were. She looked at me astonished and said my fluid levels were back up to a twelve. Just a few days prior, they had reached critical level.

She literally said that in her entire twenty-year career as a sonographer, she had never seen someone's fluid level rebuild this way. This sonographer as well as my doctors said that the only way this fluid could have refilled and remained was if somehow my bag had been resealed. That's exactly the miracle God performed for us. My sonographer said to me, "I don't know who you serve or who you pray to, but you need to come back and pray for other ladies in this situation!" She saw, firsthand, the healing power of God in our life.

It's amazing how, even with this situation, we can see that people give their opinions solely based on what they can see in that moment. My OB thought, based on what she could see with her natural eyes, that the only option we had was to give up and go home and try again. She was simply blinded by the things she could see, and gave her opinion based on those facts. Which is what many of us are guilty of. This is why it's so dangerous to give people, whose minds change like the wind or who live based on how circumstances look, the permission to give you permission. I'm so grateful that we decided to look to God and what He had to say about our situation, because He never misses! He is Alpha and Omega, so our circumstance appearing to be dire didn't cause Him to doubt in any way. **God knows that what we see in a moment is temporary.** He holds all power, and all things on Earth are subject to Him. He gives us full permission to trust in His Word, no matter how dark or bleak the situation becomes. People will say there is no hope just because your marriage, health, or job situation appears hopeless in a particular season. All the while, God could be setting you up to perform a miracle. I wonder how many miracles we've missed because we listened to the advice of others over the voice of God? How many miracles have we missed by trusting what the circumstances looked like, over what the Father has already declared?

I must tell you about one of the biggest miracles God performed while I was lying in the hospital. Remember, it was my senior year of dental school when this whole high-risk pregnancy situation emerged. God had been fast-tracking me the entire time to finish up all my requirements. I had now been in the hospital so long that graduation was right around the corner. I felt that it was a small thing to miss walking at my graduation if it would allow my son to continue to grow and mature in the womb. I received a call, not long before graduation, from one of the most amazing teachers I had during my matriculation at MCG. Dr. Ciarrocca said to me, "Jackie, you worked so hard your entire time in dental school, and I felt it was only right to put together a graduation ceremony for you."

I was floored! It was the first time in the history of my dental school's existence that they ever performed an outside graduation ceremony for a student. It blew my mind that they would do this for little ol' me. I had to be transported down in a wheelchair, and they had to agree to do the entire ceremony within fifteen minutes. My doctors did not want me to cause any complications to the baby due to having made it so far. My dean, associate dean, several faculty members, classmates, and even the keynote speaker for my class's real graduation came to the hospital to perform my ceremony. My graduation took place in the hospital chapel the day before my class graduated. In the moment where I thought I was going to have to make what I considered to be a small sacrifice, God had other plans. God took a dire moment of my life and used it to make history! My school printed an article about this historic event, and I was left utterly speechless! The fact that God, in all of His wisdom and love, would care about every detail of my journey that much—it overwhelmed me. This event caused my level of devotion only to grow deeper for Him. He made ways that no one else could make. My family was so grateful to still be able to share in such a momentous occasion, even if it had to be held in a hospital.

Reaching twenty-eight weeks gestation was literally a dream come true! Knowing there were many people who didn't expect us to make it through, to have come so far gave us so much joy. This mark seemed so unreachable when it was initially set by our high-risk doctor some seven weeks prior! At this point, I was able to get up and start walking around. She said she would even allow me to take real showers and go to the restroom. We made it to twenty-eight weeks! Everyone was elated! The excitement was short-lived due to the fact that I began to hemorrhage the same day. They tried to do another magnesium sulfate treatment, but it would not stop the contractions. At twenty-eight weeks and one day, my doctor decided to perform an emergency C-section and bring David Jace on into the world!

WE BIRTHED A MIRACLE

At 5:59 on May 27th, 2014, after sixty-three days of bed rest, our little fighter was born. He was immediately taken to the neonatal intensive care unit. They placed him on a ventilator for just a few hours and then removed it because they saw he was able to breathe on his own. He was placed on supplemental oxygen a few days later, and even went home with it. In the NICU, the fight shifted from surviving to gaining weight to become strong enough to be discharged. There were many up and down days in the NICU. Jace underwent two blood transfusions and had major difficulty gaining weight due to severe reflux that caused him not to maintain much of his caloric intake.

As a mom who had already undergone so much, I struggled greatly during this time. It was so hard to leave him many days because I longed so desperately to hold him and have him at home with me. For a long time, we were only able to hold his finger in the incubator. This progressed to us being able to hold him for ten minutes each. I remember him growing large enough to finally put on preemie clothes. It was the Fourth of July. Changing his first doll-sized diaper and even giving him his first bottle were very special moments. I remember telling the nurse the first time I changed him, "He keeps putting his hand down in my way!" She laughed and said, "Well move his hand, momma!" I was so nervous due to all the cords and how small he was. Every progression was such a huge milestone.

We had one last scare a few days before he was released. We had just left the hospital to go home for lunch when I received a call saying that they had just resuscitated Jace. They said they almost weren't able to get him back! The entire time we were in the NICU, we never encountered life-or-death scares. It was more setbacks with weight or fighting off a small infection. Therefore, this call left me stunned. We found out that a new nurse had come to the unit, and she incorrectly read the order for what his supplemental oxygen level setting was supposed to be. She turned it down way too low, and Jace began to struggle to breathe. When I tell you—the enemy gave my baby boy his best shot! Once they resuscitated him and resolved this error, he was totally fine again! After sixty-one days in the NICU, he was finally released to us. He weighed only five pounds eight ounces at that time. We were so excited to be headed to home to start a brand-new chapter, after the fight of our lives.

I left still holding on to the promise that God gave me as I laid in the hospital bed perplexed as to why all these things had suddenly happened. God said to me, "Jackie, Jace will have no remnants of prematurity!" I stood on this promise through every dark day of the journey. I was sure that God was a keeper of His Word. In hindsight, we felt privileged that God counted us worthy to bring Him this type of glory. There were so many amazing things birthed from this time. For my son to forever have this testimony as the starting point for his faith, blows me away. The lasting imprints God left on the hearts of so many doctors, nurses, and even many of my dental classmates as a result of this supernatural miracle, is powerful. He even used this trial to strengthen the faith of Travis and me! God has given me so many reasons to trust Him! He used "Made A Way" as a nationwide anthem for all those who found themselves in impossible situations. You wouldn't believe the testimonies we've heard as a result of my baby's testimony!! I'm so grateful to say that our son is living, our son is breathing! When the doctors said NO, God said YES!

Chapter Five

CHARLOTTE: New Beginnings

"Forget the former things; do not dwell on the past. See, I am doing a new thing! Now it springs up; do you not perceive it? I am making a way in the wilderness and streams in the wasteland." —Isaiah 43:18–19 NIV

HOME SWEET HOME

We started full-time life together as the Greene Family in Charlotte, North Carolina. Travis would often jokingly say that August 1, 2014, was our second wedding day, since I was still in school when we got married. I was headed home with my two guys, and I was excited to learn who I was outside of academia, as it had been such a big part of my life. I would now have the opportunity to fully appreciate being a wife and mother. Travis and I decided that I would stay at home and care for Jace for about two years before beginning my professional career. We were now residents of the South Park area in Charlotte, a place where I would only live full-time for about a year. Travis had already been in the area about two years prior to Jace and me coming.

Four days after arriving home, my little warrior Jace decided that he no longer needed his supplemental oxygen. He began to remove it out of his nose on his own, which scared us tremendously. We had not even been able to see the lung doctor at this point. After forcing the nose cannula back into his nose for about the hundredth time, I finally gave up! I didn't believe he would keep removing it if he needed it to breathe. I found out that I was exactly right! When we got to the pulmonology appointment, the lung doctor confirmed that Jace no longer needed the supplemental oxygen. It was the last thing to go as it pertained to God manifesting His promise of Jace having no remnants of prematurity.

Being a new mommy pulled on this area of permission for me. It was crucial for me to grasp that God had given me everything I needed to be the best mother to Jace. I had to become secure in that so that I wouldn't allow the voices of others to make me second-guess that I was fully equipped! The unknowns of parenting for the first time are unreal. Then, marry that uncertainty to caring for a baby who was born three months premature. I had to lean and depend on God to guide me each day.

My days in Charlotte were full of family time! Jace was the new highlight of our world. We poured ourselves into growing and maturing him. Y'all, I fed and weighed that boy so much that first year. I was determined that my baby was going to gain weight. My mom made fun of me so much, saying I was going to have Jace solid as a linebacker. It was such a beautiful season. I learned how to rest and enjoy life. It was such a time of discovery. I was privileged to be a part of *Forest Hill Church* with my husband as he served as one of the worship leaders. We absolutely adore Pastor David Chadwick as well as his beautiful wife Marilyn! They poured so much into Travis and me during our time there! It was a pure atmosphere with such a rich and thought-provoking word.

A shift came when Travis began to feel a pull to the inner-city youth. We began to serve at a church called *Have Life*, which Pastors Shomari and Jacque White lead. They took time to love on us and allowed us to serve in their young adult and prayer ministries. Here I began to see the battle emerge between fear and me. I can recall standing in the back of one of the young adult services questioning, for the first time, if I was adequate in ministry. I felt that I needed to just keep quiet. Travis was so powerful and I never wanted to interrupt or mess up his flow! So, I stayed in the background a great deal during this time, only allowing my boldness to show through here and there! I loved praying for people, so I tended to flow in one-on-one encounters. During this time of my life, I felt that the stage was only reserved for Travis, and I enjoyed standing in full support of this dynamic husband of mine. It was a very comfortable place for me. I traveled all around to watch my baby minister through music and the Word.

In March of 2015, we got hit with unexpected news. We were pregnant with baby number two. When we called to share the news, my sister-in-law asked me how I felt, and I responded that I felt indifferent. Jace was almost one; I felt as if I had shared enough time with him, but I couldn't explain why I felt so weird about this pregnancy. Neither Travis nor I responded to this pregnancy in a way that was natural to our personality. We didn't give these unusual emotions too much thought. We figured as the pregnancy progressed we would become more excited and shake whatever it was that was bothering us.

On my first doctor's appointment, the physician's assistant told me that my HCG hormone levels were low. She said not to worry because this is often the case during the first few weeks of pregnancy. I didn't allow this to bother me much either. I went back for my first sonogram a few weeks later, and I was told that there was no heartbeat. I had obviously miscarried. The strange feeling I had when we found out we were pregnant began to make sense. I was devastated. Although I didn't know how to feel initially, due to the traumatic nature of Jace's birth, I counted all life very dear. This loss definitely dealt a heavy blow. Travis and I have always felt that the baby we lost was a little girl. Through the pain, we had peace in knowing that she was now in heaven with a loving Father who would take good care of her.

I learned how common miscarriages are through this experience. Almost every mentor I have was able to give me a personal testimony of a time they had gone through the same thing. My heart grew with compassion for all of the women who have experienced the joy of hearing they're expecting, only to have to trust God with strengthening them through the process of a miscarriage. You have to make peace with the passing of a precious little one. Through much prayer and continued faith in God's goodness, He was able to strengthen my heart again. Situations like these help us to detach God's goodness from being based on a specific outcome. I recognized that regardless of how a situation turned out, I could never let go of the fact that God is still good! This realization helped me grow in my understanding of who God is and mature beyond the finite lens that I have to look through. According to the Word, we know that God will make all things: our miscarriages, our betrayals, our disappointments—somehow work for the good of those who love Him and are called according to His purpose. God doesn't cause these things, and they break His heart, but He surely has the ability to work them for our good!

I tell you proudly that I have already seen the power of this experience in my life. The times that I've been able to grab the hands of another woman who just miscarried or lost a child due to high-risk pregnancy, and say I know exactly how you feel, helps me to count it all joy! There are so many things you can't speak to with power and conviction unless you've lived it! God has most definitely allowed me to minister through the pain of this happening in my life. We overcome by the blood of the Lamb and the word of our testimony.

THE CALL

Another major life event occurred during our time in Charlotte. We received our call to pastor. Travis was away traveling and I got a call from him while he was sitting in the airport. He said to me," Baby, do you think we will ever start a church?" I laughed a little and responded by saying, "Yes, I've always known! I've just been waiting for God to tell you!" He said he received what he could only describe as a holy burden. He knew that it was from God but that the call felt weighty. That confirmation was all we needed! We set out from that moment to realize this new instruction.

The first thing God did was confirm that we had heard Him correctly. We began to pray for direction and divine instructions. We knew He said plant a church, so we began seeking Him for the name of this movement. Travis heard the word *Forward* several times, but he kept pushing it away because he felt that it couldn't be that simple. One day, as he was sitting in front of his computer, the word *Forward* come back to his spirit. He decided to look up Forward Church to see if it already existed. At the time, there was a Forward Church in Alabama. He went and clicked on the pastors' bio. You won't believe what he saw. The pastors' names were *Travis* and *Jackie* Strickland. At this point, we knew that this was definitely God confirming His call for us to pastor Forward City Church.

We had our name. The next thing on the list was the location. Travis kept feeling God tug his heart toward Columbia, South Carolina. Columbia was a place where we knew very few people, but we knew that if God said go, we had full permission to live out everything He desired for us. We began taking trips to Columbia and started to develop a core team. Travis underwent a church planter's program, and he was also in seminary at the time. God began to align people with our vision. We were off to a good start. The core team did Bible studies and read books to prepare us for the journey ahead.

I was grateful for this time in my life! It helped me realize that there is much more to life than taking tests, studying, and making good grades. I found new joy in traveling with my husband and watching my baby boy pull up and walk for the first time. It was amazing to see our lives begin to manifest all that God had been foreshadowing from the beginning. I would say that this was a true time of rest from the cares of the world. I was very inward focused on serving my family and those God blessed me to encounter. It was here that so many remnants of ambition and wanting to perform or live up to society's standards died. I was content with just being fully me, at least the parts that I knew of myself at the time. My hair issues were still present, but I did go through a really healthy season. I began wearing my hair out for the first time, and I loved it! All of my Daddy issues were gone, and I began to feel whole for the very first time. People-pleasing definitely began to loosen its grip, and I started to enjoy the emergence of my authentic self.

Trav began to feel that it was now time to shift our life to the city where we were planning to birth this church. Jace was around 14 months, and Travis's music career had not taken off yet. Financially, we were okay, but definitely not in a season of excess. We were so serious about obeying the voice of God because it was the only way we knew to live. We began discussing the option of packing up our four-bedroom home in Charlotte, placing much of our stuff in storage, and living in an apartment. This would give us time to get established in Columbia, but most of all be right inside the will of God for our lives. We were down for whatever it took. We gave God no excuses. When He spoke, we began to move.

On one of our trips to Columbia, we began house hunting just to see what was on the market. Travis and I were very funny. Even though we weren't balling it surely didn't stop us from being picky about what we desired. We went to several neighborhoods and didn't like any of their options. As we prepared to head back to Charlotte, we saw a neighborhood tucked away in our peripheral view. We made a U-turn and pulled up to this gated community. We knew from the moment we pulled up that this neighborhood was out of our price range. While sitting at the gate, I said, "Lord, please let us find our house in here!" Travis said, "in Jesus' Name!" The guard on duty told us about all the amazing amenities. She said it had a golf course, tennis court, pool, full indoor and outdoor basketball court, and even its own restaurant. We were blown away. The guard said she had never even been privileged to go back into the neighborhood.

We arrived at the sales office and told the sales representative that we wanted to see homes with basements. For the first few houses, we didn't see anything that fit us. The last house she insisted on showing us didn't have a basement. It had a third floor which would allow enough space for Travis to convert one of the bedrooms into a studio. The moment we walked into the house, we were instantly in love. We came back two days in a row to show it to my mom and find out everything we could to possibly make this house our new home. It was exactly thirty days from the day we walked into that home until we sat down with our realtor for closing. A down payment was not required due to me being eligible for a doctor's loan. The house was turnkey! It had all appliances in it when we moved in!

It pays to allow God to be the guiding voice for your life. He did that! I wonder how many ways He has desired to make for you and me alike, but we had "our plan" that we wouldn't let go. We determined how we could logically make the thing happen in our own strength, and God was trying to show us that He didn't need our strength. Nothing about this house situation made sense in the natural! God showed us what happens when we sit back and watch Him work. I'm grateful we had determined in our hearts to obey, no matter the sacrifice. It was this heart posture that walked us right into all that God desired for us. We were off to Columbia, South Carolina.

Chapter Six

COLUMBIA: New Levels

"As Scripture says, 'Anyone who believes in him will never be put to shame.'" —Romans 10:11

MOVING FORWARD

Listen! We had no idea what we were heading toward when we said "yes" to moving to Columbia to start Forward City Church. God has absolutely blown us away in our short time here. When we relocated, David Jace was 15 months. The plan was for me to begin work in dentistry. Due to some unexpected things being exposed about the job I had been offered, Travis and I decided not to proceed forward with it. The arrangements for Jace to start attending day care here in Columbia were already set. However, having my child at this particular day care only lasted for eight days. The final straw was when I went in to pick him up, and I had to inform the teacher that a little girl was closed in the cabinet. Let's just say, that was the last day they ever saw David Jace. So now, it was back to me caring for Jace full-time at home.

Travis' music career had completely taken off. On the heels of being asked to perform at Bishop T. D. Jakes's, *Pastors and Leadership*

Conference, our life shifted into another dimension. God used Travis in dynamic ways at the conference, and the world who had known much of his music now knew the artist attached to this fresh sound. "Intentional," Travis's single, went number one, followed by "Made a Way" and then *The Hill* album! The booking requests were coming nonstop. As a result, Travis was doing a lot of traveling. Amidst all of this, we were pushing full steam ahead with training, facilitating Bible studies, and building morale with our core team for the church. We had also launched our Forward City Nights of Worship on the Benedict College campus in September of 2015. One of our major mission fields as a church is college students. We began by going to the students to become an established resource and to let them know that we would be in the city permanently.

These Nights of Worship were flooded with students and others from the community who heard about the impact that was happening each month we came. Hundreds of students were responding to the invitation for salvation, and others were being provided the opportunity to encounter God in a way they never had before. A huge following for our church plant was created from these radical moments with God. We were gearing up for our Monday night *Worship and Word* encounters. They were set to start in April of 2016, followed by our launch of Sunday services on August 21st, 2016! The momentum we were seeing even before our official launch was so encouraging.

Can I just say on the onset that the process of raising such a young family, while planting a brand-new church, and in my case stepping into full-time ministry for the first time, was absolutely that—a PROCESS?! The permission concept demanded attention as I began to walk this journey out with God. It seemed as if everything I had been content with believing or even saw as my norm, God came to check. I was hearing over and over, "No baby, that thing you have been basing your life around actually isn't true. Will you let Me show you your truth?" I had no idea answering Yes to this invitation would take me to some very high highs and very low lows.

God is so gracious in that He takes His time with us once we accept the invitation to go higher. We began our Monday night *Worship and Word* services downtown at a place called Agape. Our first service was so intimate yet powerful. We were only there about three months, and in that time, we had to expand twice within this building to hold all the people who began showing up consistently. I remember like yesterday, right before we were getting ready to begin one of these services, Travis walked up to me and said, "I'm going to have you do the welcome tonight after we end worship!" He said it so nonchalantly and just kept on moving to the next thing on his to-do list.

When I tell y'all—my mind began moving a thousand miles a minute, and my heart wouldn't stop racing. I was totally out of whack internally, and he'd only asked me to say a welcome. I'm not quite sure why this unnerved me so badly, but one thing I knew was I had to get to my mom. She has always been a voice that helps center me and brings me back to peace. The moment she came through the doors, I took off in her direction. I took her to the back to explain to her how I didn't even feel ready to say a welcome. I was crying profusely, mainly because I was disappointed in myself for feeling the way I did in that moment. I said things like, "Jackie, how are you going to have Travis calling you a lead pastor alongside him, and you can't even get up and say a welcome! You are a doctor for pete's sake, and you can't even say a welcome! All your life people have spoken over and over about how much potential you have, but saying a welcome has you in a back room crying! What in the world are you going to do when God asks you to preach your first sermon?" Just the thought of that day left me completely overwhelmed and defeated!

My mom has always been so patient with me. Her voice cut through the noise of all these tormenting thoughts as she began to pray God's Word over me. She wasn't moved by my tears or even my doubts! God's truth was strength for me in this time of weakness! His truth will remind you of what He has already declared and destroy the grip of others' opinions! By the time I walked back out to give that welcome, I felt strong internally! I'm sure I spoke really fast and didn't perform perfectly according to man, but the fact that I didn't back down and obeyed God was perfection in His eyes.

It's amazing how, in moments that seem so small in our lives, there can be so much happening spiritually of which we are unaware. What I realized, in reflection, is that although it seemed to just be a welcome in the natural, God was shifting me into a new dimension of my call. I was approaching a new life of God using the voice that I hadn't fully found, but I was ok with giving it to Him even in an infantile stage. I have referenced this night more times than I can count. Each one of my mentees knows this story by heart because it always comes up when I am daring them to live their truth as well. I'm grateful that I lived through moments like this one. It helped produce the understanding and compassion necessary to equip my spiritual sons and daughters no matter what stage they are in when they arrive to us. God established a faith stone here in a moment when I felt most inadequate. He proved to me that He was sure about me when He called me, and He didn't need my strength to fulfill this call on my life. All He needed was my Yes! God desires our willingness to not give up or live beneath the place He has called us. For too long, the possibility of failure or not being perfect for man stopped me from even trying. This night turned out to be amazing, and it was pivotal in my journey forward.

We were now at our official launch day for Forward City Church. On August 21, 2016, we stood inside of all the prayers and prophecies that so many people had released. We had now relocated to a loft in the Columbia Museum of Arts to hold our Sunday services. The room was filled with excitement! We had family and friends from all over the United States, packed into this loft area. There was so much anticipation for all that God would do during this inaugural service. I remember being so big that I felt I was going to pop. I was one month away from giving birth to our second baby boy!

God moved so mightily at this service. Travis preached a message entitled "Scratched!" This message centered around the understanding that scratches will be endured while obeying the instruction of the Lord. The question then becomes *How do we handle living persecuted for the sake of obeying God?* We are challenged to gain the perspective of the Apostles. They literally counted it an honor to be worthy enough to suffer for the sake of Christ! It was incredible to see the hand of God demonstrated in such a dynamic way. We made it through our first service! We were ecstatic!

Sunday after Sunday, the momentum of this Forward movement continued to grow. We were witnessing more and more salvations. Our number of Forward City partners was continuously increasing. We had numerous first-time guests, and it was clear that our desire for our church to be a real hospital and place of freedom was translating. We were off to a dynamic start.

THE CHAMP IS HERE!

In our personal life, I had just given birth to our second baby boy, Travis Joshua, better known as "Champ!" Before we go any further, I have to take a moment to tell you about how we found out that we were expecting. It is such an incredible story. It was February of 2016 when we were surprised and relieved by the news of expecting a new baby. I had been feeling horrible for so long. It was *Stellar Awards* weekend, and we were gearing up to head back home. My best friend, Keshia, and I decided that it only made sense to take one more pregnancy test even though I had taken one a few weeks prior and had gotten a negative result. I was still feeling so sick, so we needed to be sure. We spontaneously decided to go into a CVS and take a test. I was craving cheese puffs, so we told Travis and his team that we would be right back. We went in, grabbed the cheese puffs, and I took the test while in the store. I came out of the restroom with *Big News*. The test was positive! We were so excited and Keshia kept repeating, "Jack, I knew it!"

I now had the pleasure of explaining to my husband that while I was out buying cheese puffs, I found out that I was having another one of his babies! Talk about an interesting trip to CVS! Travis and his best friend, Kobie, had a blast with the news! We called all of our family to share the news! The Greene family had a lot of new things on the horizon.

The awaited day of Josh's delivery was here. On September 27, 2016, at 8:16 a.m. my little Champ entered the world! It was such a joyous occasion. Jace was so happy to have a little brother, and Travis was a proud father. Although they took him at thirty-seven weeks, he was a healthy seven-pound, nine-ounce baby! Due to Josh's birth not being as traumatic, I was able to fully experience things as a mother that I wasn't able to do with Jace. I discovered the beautiful bonding that comes through nursing as well as the joy of taking your baby home with you when you leave the hospital. The normalcy was a true gift to our family based on our prior history. We were so thrilled to bring Josh home!

While I was at home healing from the C-section and settling into life at home with our new bundle of joy, God took me through a very unsettling season. I was in a time of great reflection. I was up and down all night nursing, and if I were honest, I felt like I was on an island alone. As a family—be it my husband, mom, brother, sister-in-law, or even my best friend, everyone was heavily involved in the church. It felt as if nothing else existed in life except our new church.

I can recall crying at home on my floor hoping that when the family got home that everyone's conversation wouldn't center around something about the church. Although we were in need of a much better balance between ministry life and family time, that wasn't the whole story. Through prayer and crying out to God, I came to recognize that a lot of the emotions had more to do with me than anything externally! I had underlying issues that made me open to these advances of the enemy. He told me during this time at home, "See, Jackie, nobody cares about you and the new baby, but you! Nobody at the church even misses you. It's cool if you're there, but you're definitely not a necessity. As long as Forward City has Pastor Travis, then they are absolutely great! They don't even know how to address you. Pastor? First Lady? Travis Greene's wife?" There were so many questions and doubts in my heart about this new phase we had just stepped into.

I'm sure, reading some of these thoughts, you can see that I was sleep deprived, still hormonal, and home with way too much idle time on my hands. You might imagine the recipe for disaster and low self-worth that I was living through. I was crying myself to sleep, during the times that I did get sleep, and keeping all of these thoughts and emotions bottled inside. One reason I held it all in was because I didn't want to face the fact that I felt this way. Secondly, I felt that it was horrible to feel this way about the blessing of Forward City Church. Lastly, I knew Travis had a million things on him already, so I did my best not to weigh him down with my emotions. I'm sure every woman married to a man working in ministry knows the fullness of my last statement in a way no one else does. We try to hold it all together thinking that we are helping things, don't we? Then, it all comes roaring out!

REAL TALK. REAL WORK.

All that I've just shared might alarm anyone reading this who is preparing to enter ministry, especially my fellow sisters in Christ. Let me just say, facing truth always works out for your good. All of those emotions helped me to uncover the lies and find true freedom. God makes no mistakes when He calls us. Do not fear, my sister! It was a hard thing to stand secure in knowing what the Father had said about me when, to my side, I had someone who seemed to have this ministry thing all figured out already! He is great at everything, which made me critique myself even harder! His greatness in ministry challenged me up in the best way but caused me to doubt, too. I am so very grateful for the Father allowing me this time of discomfort. It forced me to confront things in myself that I never had the courage to face in the prior seasons.

What God revealed as I cried out during these times was truth. Underneath all of the surface things that I used as an easy scapegoat for anger or frustration, the fact that I was still not fully living my truth was my biggest disgruntlement. I finally faced the fact that, for way too long, I had been hitting the same ceiling called *Woman of God, you've got so much potential!* I was absolutely sick of *potential*! I was, in every way, over just being full of potential. Instead of continuing to have a pity party, I got to work. I stopped crying about the fact that I desired a spiritual mentor to invest in me and to cultivate all this potential inside of me that everybody saw. I began to live FORWARD! I submitted my life to the guidance and authority of the Holy Spirit, and I began to ask Him to do in my life what the Word says He desires to do: guide, teach, and counsel me!

This revelation gave rise to my own personal platform where I began to share my journey of truth with other women as an aid to help them live FORWARD! I gathered some of the baddest girls on the planet to help me execute the vision that was now burning in my heart. I wanted to empower women to live beyond the pitfalls, past mistakes, and excuses of fear and inadequacy. I recognize that we will have moments that knock us down and delay us, but we have to decide to get back up and continue FORWARD. We will be women of progression! We will no longer sit around and just dream big dreams. We will be a people of REAL TALK and REAL WORK! We will be women who do the internal work necessary to produce the outward and forward motion necessary to see RESULTS! I wanted to see RESULTS, not potential, and I was going to push every girl in my path to make that same choice!

You see, when you actually begin to confront the things going on inside of you, you are able to more accurately see the things around you! It is why it's so vital to find your truth! As I began the step-by-step process of walking toward the life that God had already given me full permission to live, all the superficial distractions that the enemy wanted me to be upset about faded away! The more I became satisfied with me, the more I no longer needed anyone to make me feel needed. I knew what the Father called me—*a Forward Woman, a BRAVE and BAD Girl, a Daughter, and Priceless*—so the label other people chose didn't matter! I was never hung up on titles. My struggles with inadequacy in the area of ministry made me think what people called me equated to validation. I thought if someone viewed me as a pastor like they did Travis, then *Hey, maybe I was good enough*! If, on the other hand, they only saw me as First Lady, due to the negative connotations I had been exposed to with that title, I felt that they only expected me to be some pretty trophy wife with no substance or power! First Lady, for me, carried a superficial connotation making me cringe inside because I didn't see myself that way! Let me be clear, I know that not everyone views the term that way; it was simply my perspective based on things I had seen and heard during my life's journey. At the end of the day, no title defines you or your value. You define the title, and that's the place I landed as I stepped into this Forward season.

My frustrations with adding the additional focus of Forward City to our lives dissipated when I found fulfillment. I was living inside of my brand-new life of walking confidently in my call! I still work hard to help maintain a healthy family life outside of what's going on with the ministry, but I'm able to help facilitate this for my family in a healthy way now that I'm whole. Rather than crying, assuming, or nagging, I often just invite Travis to come home and have dinner with the boys and me if we're missing him! I will set up a facial and couples massage date for the two of us, if I can tell we need some time to reconnect. Ladies, there are ways to get the desired results in your marriage and family outside of nagging or being manipulative or angry. Submit your life to the guidance of the Holy Spirit, and He will turn what you were just seeing as a negative into a positive. The way the Holy Spirit will cause you to take self-inventory and begin to pray prayers to help support and encourage your spouse will blow your mind. Try it! I'm telling you it works!

All this revelation came out of a decision to begin living Forward in my thinking and to stretch beyond what was comfortable. The heights I would reach just by resting in the hands of the Father are beyond words! The moment I said *Yes*, God pushed me hard and fast! I made the decision to start doing internal work in October or November. By December, my team and I successfully hosted our very first women's event called *EXHALE*! It was incredible! I never imagined that I was capable of creating this type of safe environment for women of all backgrounds to come together and release! After carrying the weight of the world—the pressure of mothering, careers, and relationships—it is so necessary for women to have safe places to let go. We worshiped, prayed, had moments of transparency, cut up a little, and most of all, each lady left changed! I was blown away at what happens when you unleash potential into the hands of God! The success of this encounter only fueled my passion to become more free! I began to recognize, even at this stage, that **FREE people FREE people**!

My husband, who is my greatest coach, loves to aid the Holy Spirit in launching me out into water too deep for me to stand up in. The same weekend as *Exhale*, he decided that it was time for me to preach my first sermon at Forward City Church. This also happened to be the very first sermon of my life in a pulpit! I preached all the time to my friend circle, but God was ushering me to a whole new level. In one weekend, God did all this. You wouldn't believe the title of my sermon that Sunday! It was entitled "GIVE ME FAITH!" Not only was I preaching for the first time, but it was also the first Sunday Travis ever missed at the church. He left me to hold it all down. Talk about needing faith! In my head I thought, "Lord, I just gave You my Yes like two months ago. Are You sure I'm ready for all of this?" He made clear that His answer to that question was Yes! He continued to call my name over and over, to give Him one Yes, after the next Yes, that led to the next Yes. I know my delivery wasn't the most polished that Sunday. There were many things, when I listened back, that I would have loved to change. Despite the imperfections, I was sure that God was well pleased by the way He filled the room! He gave me all the faith I needed. Romans 10:11 is the scripture that got me started and keeps me going as I approach every new door that feels bigger than I am. If I put my trust in the Lord, then I will not be disappointed. I stand on that Word as my promise!

My next big faith moment was my first photo shoot that December. This shoot was in preparation for the launch of my very own website. I was so uncomfortable at the beginning. I had no idea how difficult so many things were that I had seen Travis do effortlessly. The beautiful thing about God in His wisdom is that He didn't send Travis through artist development training just for him. He had me in mind. Travis literally came on set, tickled me, made silly faces, and had them play music to help loosen me up. As a result, the shoot turned out a phenomenal success. I decided to mention this part in the book because we often see pictures posted on social media and automatically think people have it all together. I wanted to dispel this misconception to highlight that many of your greatest inspirations on social media are no different than you. They have to fight fear, contend with moments of doubt, and push to reach every new level of faith. I pray that this transparency helps you realize that you too can do the thing God has placed in your heart if you just dare to try!

We have now made it to the year 2017! I was fully committed to shedding all the remaining layers in my life. I wanted to do away with anything that held the potential to land me back in a place of immobility. I have always had a huge longing to become all that God desired me to be. I was very focused on this quest as we began 2017. That January, I had the pleasure of speaking at our *Night of Worship* at Columbia College (all-women's college). This gathering was another defining moment in ministry for me. That night, I felt as if God was daring me to go on stage and speak from my heart. Although I had prepared notes and worked through exactly what I wanted to say, I had learned how much it pays to obey God rather than stick to your own agenda. The whole message centered around letting go of the counterfeit version of yourself, the person we create in an attempt to please others. I challenged them to embrace the "you" that God created. This "you" is the version that God adores. When it came time for the altar call (an invitation for prayer in response to this challenge), the entire auditorium came down front. God showed me through this, that it is He who knows just the way to touch the hearts of those He created. Oftentimes, in our own wisdom or based on a past experience of how God moved, we think that we have figured Him out. These kinds of moments help remind us to allow God to guide us every time.

A side note that is too funny not to include—In my excitement of finally being free, I humiliated myself. Before it was time to go in to start the night of worship, I was out in the lobby greeting people. I was having an amazing time when I decided that it was time for me to head back to my green room before things started. In order to get to this green room, I had to enter a doorway located between two glass frames. I'm sure you can tell by now that this scenario is not going to end well. I began to head toward this entrance, or so I thought. There were people everywhere. Some people were on the same side of the door frame as I was, and others were on the side I was approaching. I walked straight into one of the glass frames, with no room to play it off! I was so embarrassed! I kept my head down and continued to walk toward the green room, acknowledging no one who stood around laughing at me. Nonetheless, it was an incredible night, one that I will never forget!

It was now time to launch my brand-new website! It was such an exciting feeling to invite people into my world. This site gave legs to the Forward Woman Movement by allowing other women to join and begin to follow all things Forward. They were able to access clips of my speaking engagements, participate in monthly challenges, and even read my blogs. The response was overwhelming, and it felt good to see more *Real Work* being established. Launching this website also opened the door for several other speaking engagements. The privilege to share my heart with other ladies meant everything to me.

I remember my very first speaking engagement after launching my site. I had been invited to the *Victorious Secrets* conference in Virginia. This event was one to remember. What stood out to me most was the fact that I didn't feel afraid at all! I actually felt prepared for the moment. God is so wise in His ability to prepare us while we are completely unaware of being groomed. As I traveled all around the world supporting my husband, I had no idea that these trips were training grounds for the day I would arrive to different places for my own engagements. I knew just what to expect when it came to travel, lobby calls, and so many other engagement-related things. I also had my best friend Keshia with me running point as my operations manager.

The demographic of my audience for this event was predominantly African. I feel that there was so much intention in God sending me to a place of kindred spirits for my first event. As a young lady who had grown up in America with African heritage by way of my father, I had always had so many questions about which of my characteristics came from my African people. This event exposed me to two predominant traits that many Africans exhibit. They are very confident and fiery. When I came home, I remember telling Travis and Norman that being among my African people had awakened this greater level of assurance of who I was in Christ. Through this encounter, I realized that I had full permission to be passionate and fiery because it was true to who I really am!

I'm not sure if the picture is becoming clear, but it felt like I was in this ready-made story. Month after month upon giving my *Yes*, the Father began to pour more and more fuel on my fire! About two months later, I was set to preach at Forward City. When I woke up that morning, the understanding of my permission being granted by the Father was blazing in me! I decided that morning that I wanted to wear a black sleeveless dress with a white collar, black leggings, and complete the look with my black-and-white Chuck Taylors. This dress had pockets! If anybody knows how much I love dresses with pockets, it's my stylist Salihah (@stylemesalihah)! Check her out; she's bomb!

That Sunday, I also desired to preach with my cell phone. As I was getting acclimated to preaching, I often felt like my iPad held me back. I wanted to be fully free! I preached a message called *The Power of One*. Many of you may know it as the "Pancake Mix" message. It is still one of my greatest messages to date, in my book! I loved the freedom I felt the day I chose to live in the comfort of my own skin and do things the way I truly wanted! I blew up the box that day and decided it was too small to contain me!

THE REBIRTH OF DR. JG

God didn't stop with producing greater levels of freedom in my preaching. What He decided to do next absolutely changed the game FOREVER! Insert the day He came for one of my greatest covers! Although I had been wearing wigs intermittently, the experimenting with my natural hair during this season had begun! I wanted to slay this "hair issues" giant badly! I began looking for a stylist who was well-educated about natural hair and one who could possibly bring definition to my natural curl pattern. My first call was to Keshia, who is my go-to for all things related to natural hair. She recommended that I try this young lady named Flo who is a *Deva Curl* specialist here in the Columbia area.

This natural hair quest led to my second appointment where I was sitting in Flo's chair. I lost my mind and said the words and did the thing I didn't think I would ever be brave enough to do. I said, "Flo, let's cut it off!" I had recently seen a cut on Taraji P. Henson that I felt confident I could rock. By confident, I mean I saw myself fully rocking this look in my head but never believed that it would be my reality. I had also told no one in my inner circle about this new look that was burning in me to try—not Travis, my mom, Keshia, Crystal, no one! While sitting in this chair asking Flo at least one million questions, I had a moment of clarity. I realized that if I could overcome this hurdle, then I was sure I could do anything. I would not only be slaying the giant of "hair issues" but I would also be sending a real heavy blow to this need to always have *permission*. To take this type of step while my husband was away in Canada and not have one of my friends right there coaching was monumental! I did it! I shoved every excuse that came at me right under my feet, and I made a decision to live my truth in every aspect. That first Saturday of August, I walked out of that shop as a new woman.

This new cut provoked even greater levels of freedom, boldness, and passion! This forced my team and me to completely relaunch the *DrJG* website! We added new content based on some of my areas of huge passion: *Stable Relationships, True Self-Worth,* and *Persistent Faith during High-Risk Pregnancies.* It was clear that the message within these focus points was being heard loudly and clearly as the following continued to exponentially grow. I continued to travel for a few speaking engagements and I also hosted my second *Exhale* event.

It seemed surreal to see all the things God had accomplished in just a year's time. We were back to the time where I had done my first event the year prior. *Exhale 2017* more than doubled in size! I expanded the vision and we executed this event with an even higher standard of excellence. The number of testimonies I received about the impact from *Exhale 2017,* as well as several ladies coming to join the Forward City family due to attending this event, was mind-blowing. My team worked diligently, and I was so pleased with the outcome of *Exhale 2017*! We closed 2017 with a bang!

As a church, we brought the new year in declaring that we had access, keys, no barriers, and authority according to Matthew 16:19. I was fired up and ready to obey every new instruction of the Lord. As it pertains to *DrJG,* at the start of the year I really felt the Lord asking me to be still. I didn't fully understand the instruction. But I felt He was asking me not to go into a lot of planning for new initiatives and things to accomplish. I sensed that He was preparing my very own lane for me, and it would be through this vehicle that I would continue to grow and make Kingdom impact.

In January, we launched our very first monthly *Dig Deep* women's Bible study! From the moment I stepped into the atmosphere that night, I knew that this was exactly why God had been telling me to be still. Our *Dig Deep* encounters are like no other. They are completely out of the box. It is a mixture of free prophetic worship, prayer, dance, spoken word, digging into the Word, and a time for women of all types to find their voices. It is a sacred time every third Friday in the city of Columbia, for women near and far to come be poured into.

Dig Deep gives me the opportunity to grow in my gift as a visionary, teacher, preacher, and pastor. Each month, it is my delight to present my ladies with something fresh and ripe to provoke change. Due to being able to prepare messages and teach the Word more often, I have been blown away at the amount of growth God has provided in my own personal life. I love this new ministry opportunity because I'm able to fully express whatever the heartbeat of God has been in my life that month with my ladies! They are My BAD Girls!

Dig Deep was not the only new thing that approached on the horizon of the new year. In January, God opened the door for me to finally begin pouring my love into the area of dentistry. Due to graduating in 2014 and not beginning to practice until 2018, I was fortunate to spend about two months getting acclimated to the whole dental world all over again. The Davis family took me under their wing, then introduced me to Dr. Dingle who extended this same level of mentorship.

I have now joined the Davis and Dingle Family Dentistry team as an Associate Dentist and have been practicing dentistry twice a week! The joy that has come from this new chapter of my life is somewhat hard to articulate. Being able to give a hug, peace, knowledge, care, alleviate pain, and render professional services in one setting is extremely unique and totally what I'm about! This step for me was one that took me being sure of the permission I had been granted by God. Due to making the decision to approach my professional career from a non- traditional aspect, I had not touched a patient in over three years. I had to be sure that God would guide me into becoming fully proficient in all areas of dentistry, so that I would be able to provide my patients with the utmost care. This was very important to me. It was a bit scary in the beginning, but God calmed all my fears by showing me how much I actually remembered. Not only did He do that, but

He placed me within an organization where I would be led by two of the most amazing senior doctors in the dental profession. They took my hand and helped me to feel as if I never missed a day. God is so faithful!

It is very important to me to maintain the freedom to be fluid with the leading of the Holy Spirit, as to when I work in the dental profession. I know that this ability would not even be possible if my identity were wrapped in being a doctor. I have always desired for dentistry to be a part of my life, but for it not to *be* my life. As I desire with all things. With the concept of permission, it is so important that we hold on to the freedom to go against the social norms of how everybody else in our profession does things. God did not create us to be like everybody else, and had I let the questions of family and friends pressure me into feeling obligated to do dentistry full-time, I would have missed out on so many other amazing things God had planned for me.

I have been able to bring a great level of stability to our household because of not working full-time and being available to be at home with our children to nurture them. The opportunity to focus on cultivating my spiritual gifts has also been present, along with the ability to travel and empower women from all different walks of life. If you are a woman who is struggling with the decision to slow your pace, or maybe even stop working in a particular career for a season, know that you have permission to do that if that is what you are being spiritually led to do. There is so much freedom in not being boxed in!

God has expanded the borders of all that the *DrJG* platform represents! I love how He does things! I never would've believed, as I was lying on my floor crying out to break through the glass ceiling of potential, that all I have written to you was on the other side. I wonder what's on the other side of you choosing to give up this need to have everyone approve or validate who God has already given you permission to be? What giants stand in the way of your truth? Like David, you, too, have the power to become a giant-slayer when you allow the Father to empower you!

I pray, through my story, you have been persuaded to live your truth! You must fight to eradicate the need to have others say what the Father has already declared about you. God has been singing the same song over you your entire life. Some seasons we are more in tune to hear it! I pray that you will return back to the God-created version of yourself. The "you" untainted by the pressures and opinions of the outside world! I pray that you will live to delight in the smile of your Father in heaven! After closing this book, you have the opportunity to open a new chapter of your own life story. The one that is truth. The one that is real. The one that is authentic. My dear friend, you have full PERMISSION! I DARE YOU TO LIVE IN IT!

STATEMENT OF PERMISSION

Permission! Man, this concept has revolutionized my life. I can't tell you the number of times in the past few weeks, when faced with a thought of bondage, I have said, "Oh, so you need permission again?!" Immediately, I found myself free! There is so much power in recognizing that the internal questioning based on the hypotheticals of others' opinions is the epitome of asking for permission! The more I have come to recognize this behavior, the more skilled I have become at shutting it down! Owning my permission from my Daddy in heaven has shut down the questions of inadequacy. My permission broke the back of fear and propelled me to live my best life! We start on this journey knowing that we have full permission, only to become distracted by the thoughts and emotions of others so much that we lose grip of what we once knew. We go through a process of reversing God's truth and needing to have everyone approve and validate our choices. Staying the course lands you back at the place of firmly owning the words that the Father has spoken specifically about you! Permission helped me to own that nobody could be a better wife and mother to my three kings! It settled the fact that I am one fast-talking, fiery, anointed preacher! I realize that although I am a pastor who loves and leads well, my leading won't look like that of anybody else. It reverses the idea that my uniqueness is a disqualifier and helps me to see that it is why I am qualified. If I did it exactly like anyone else, what need would there be for me? I settled the fact that although I'm brilliant, I'm also from Sandersville, which gives me a little country flavor of which I'm very proud! I love that I own what I wear, how I do my hair, and my option to get glammed up or chill all the way down! To know that none of these things have possession over me means everything! I am free from hair issues and daddy issues! I am a woman who OWNS her PERMISSION!

What is your statement of permission? What have you decided to fully embrace about yourself that you once questioned? Have you come to the place where you dare to LIVE your truth? Read my last question carefully! I don't want you to just KNOW your truth; that's just potential! The moment you begin to LIVE your truth, you become unstoppable! I dare you to LIVE! Permission is yours!

CPSIA information can be obtained
at www.ICGtesting.com
Printed in the USA
BVHW091759190422
634698BV00016B/991/J

9 780578 430867